THIS FRIGHTFUL COLORING BOOK
BELONGS TO:

_____

COPYRIGHT © 2020 CREATIVE COLORING CORNER
All rights reserved.

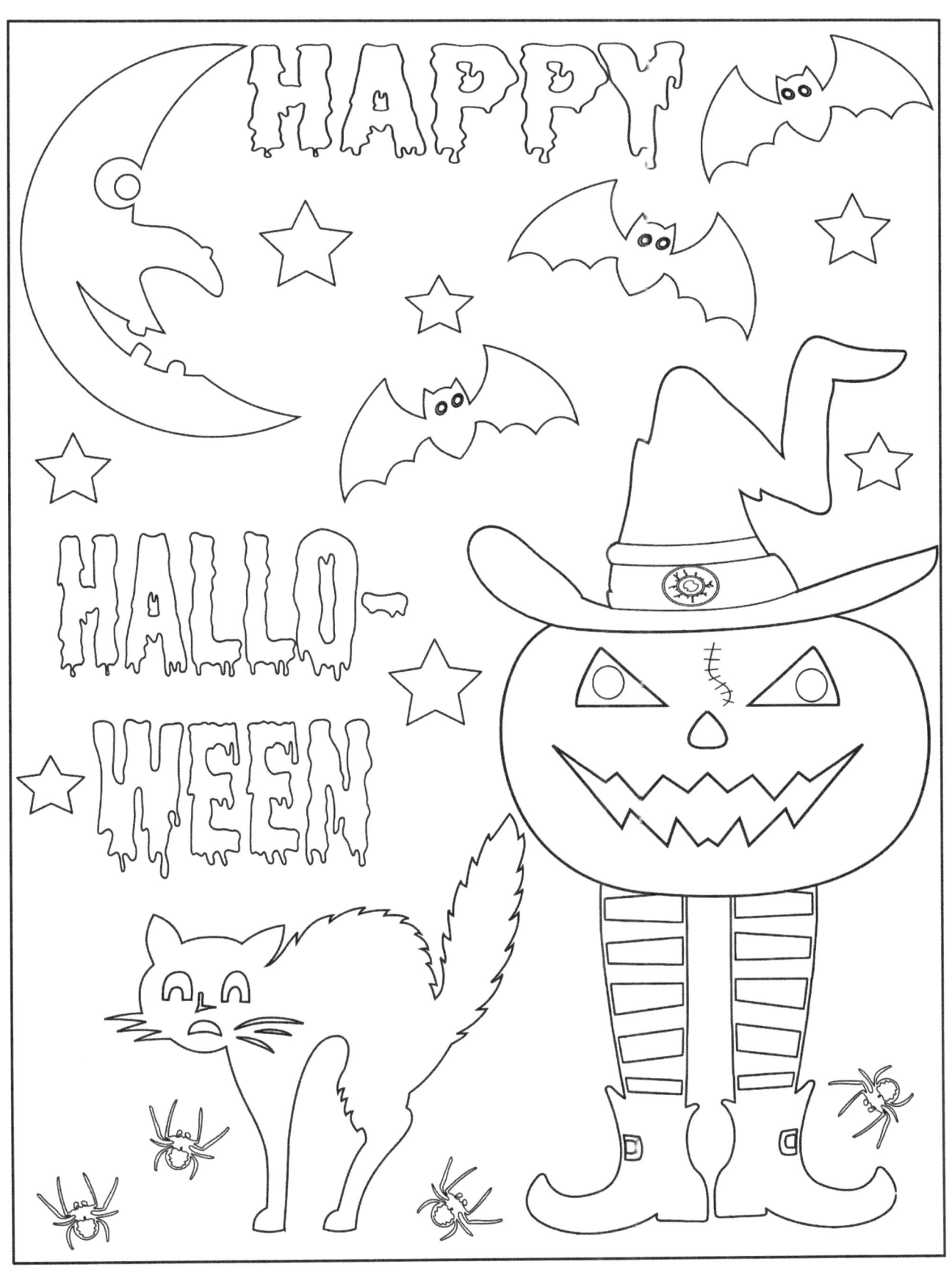

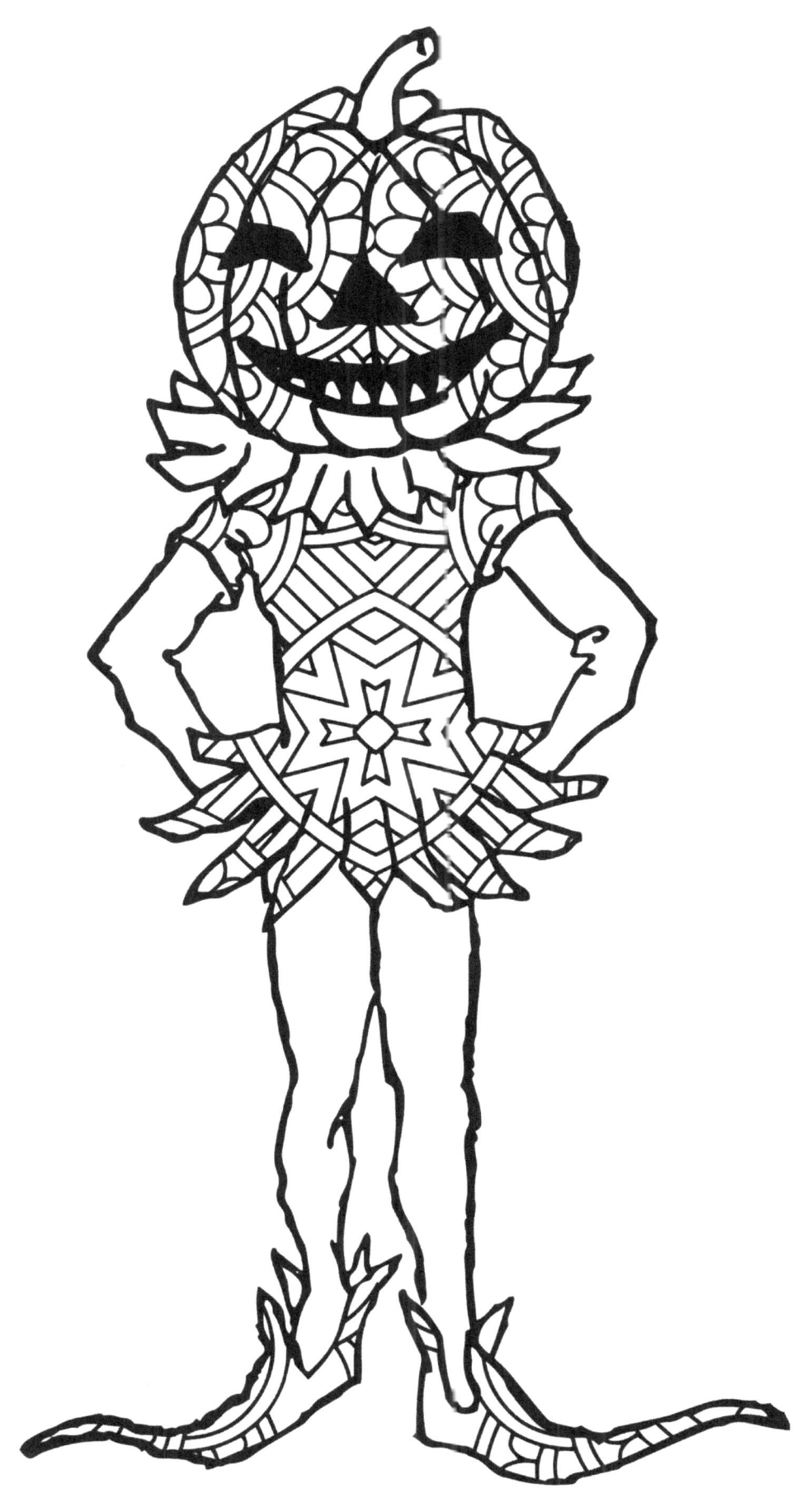

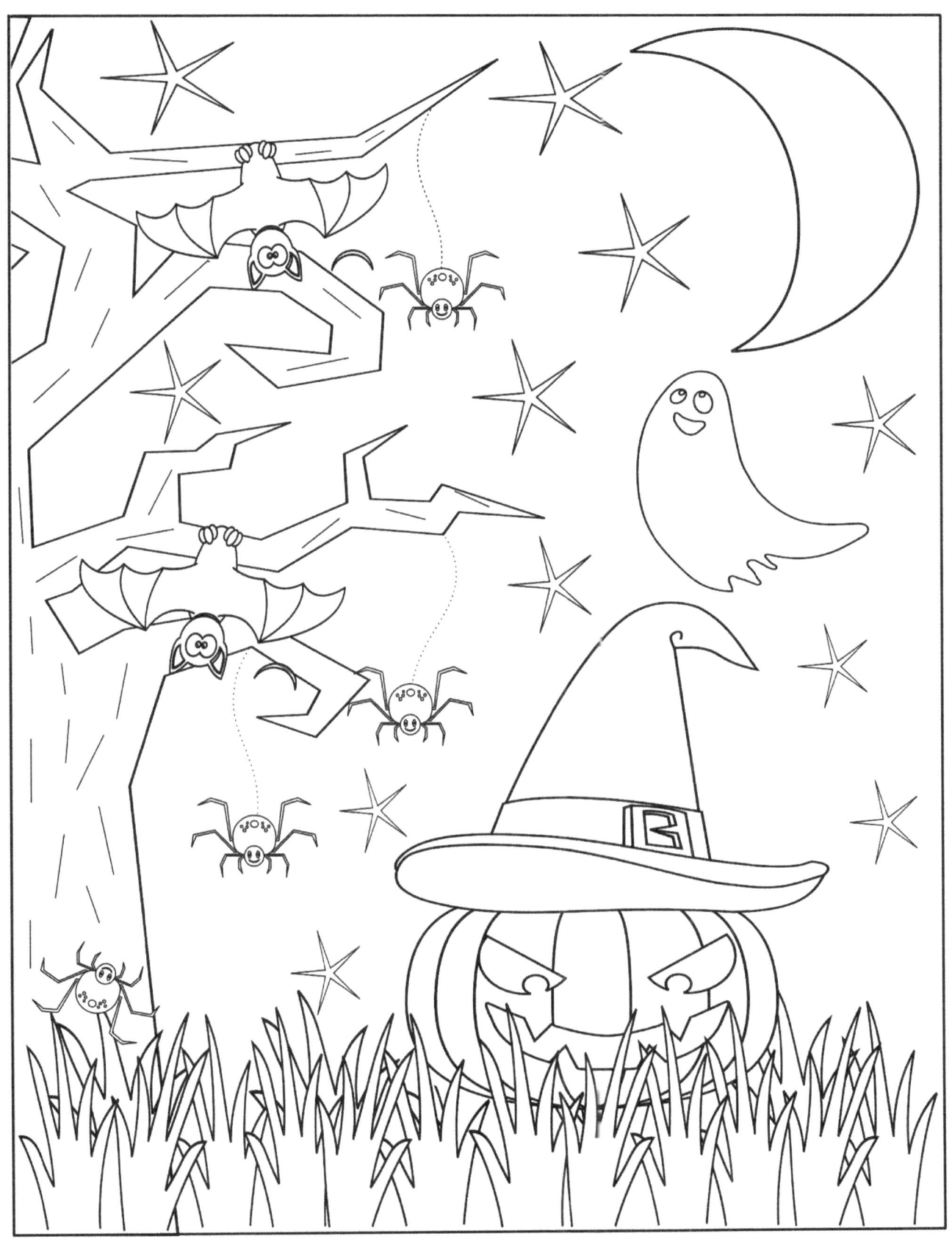

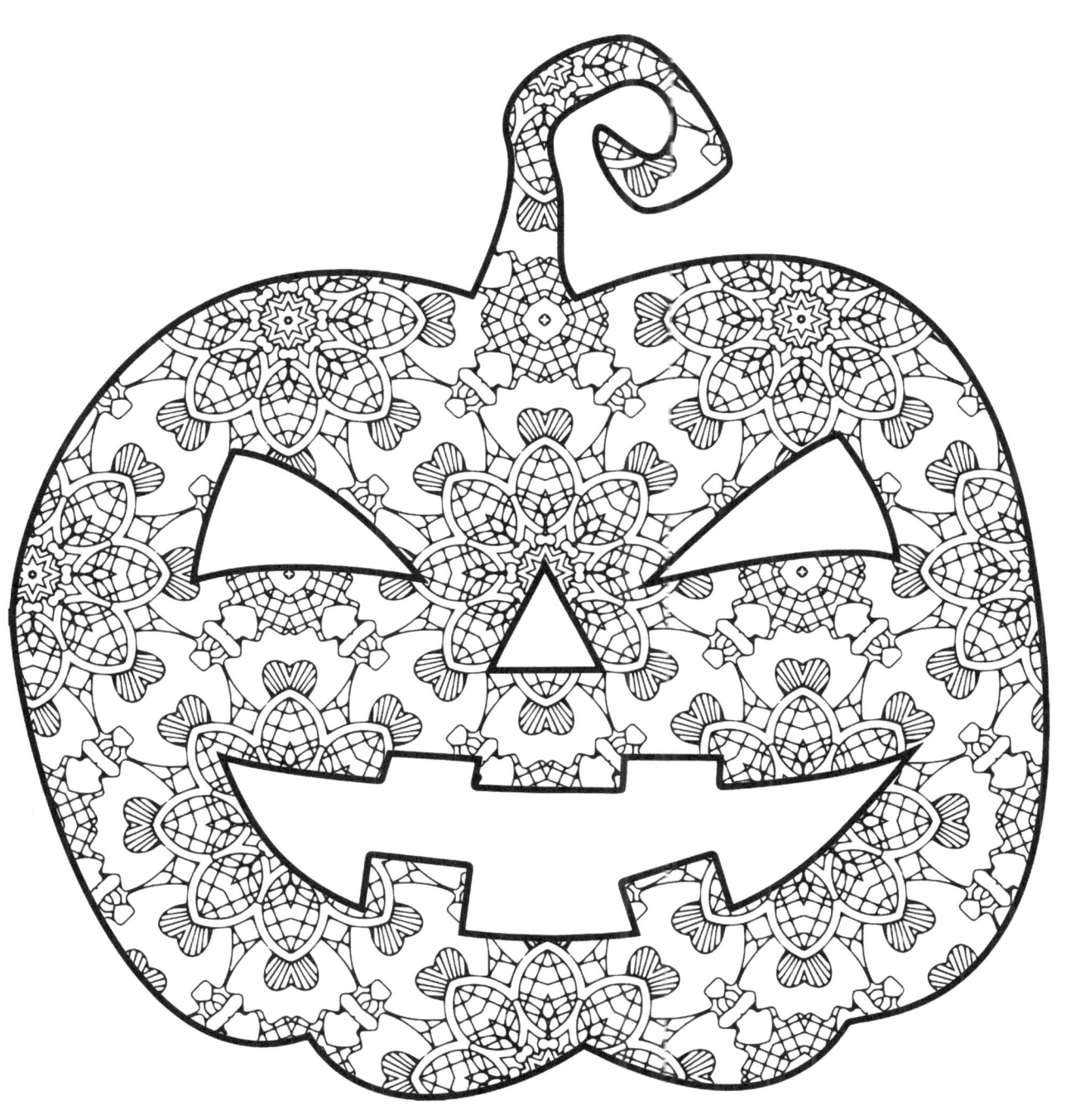

THERE IS MAGIC IN THE NIGHT
WHEN THE PUMPKINS GLOW BY MOONLIGHT

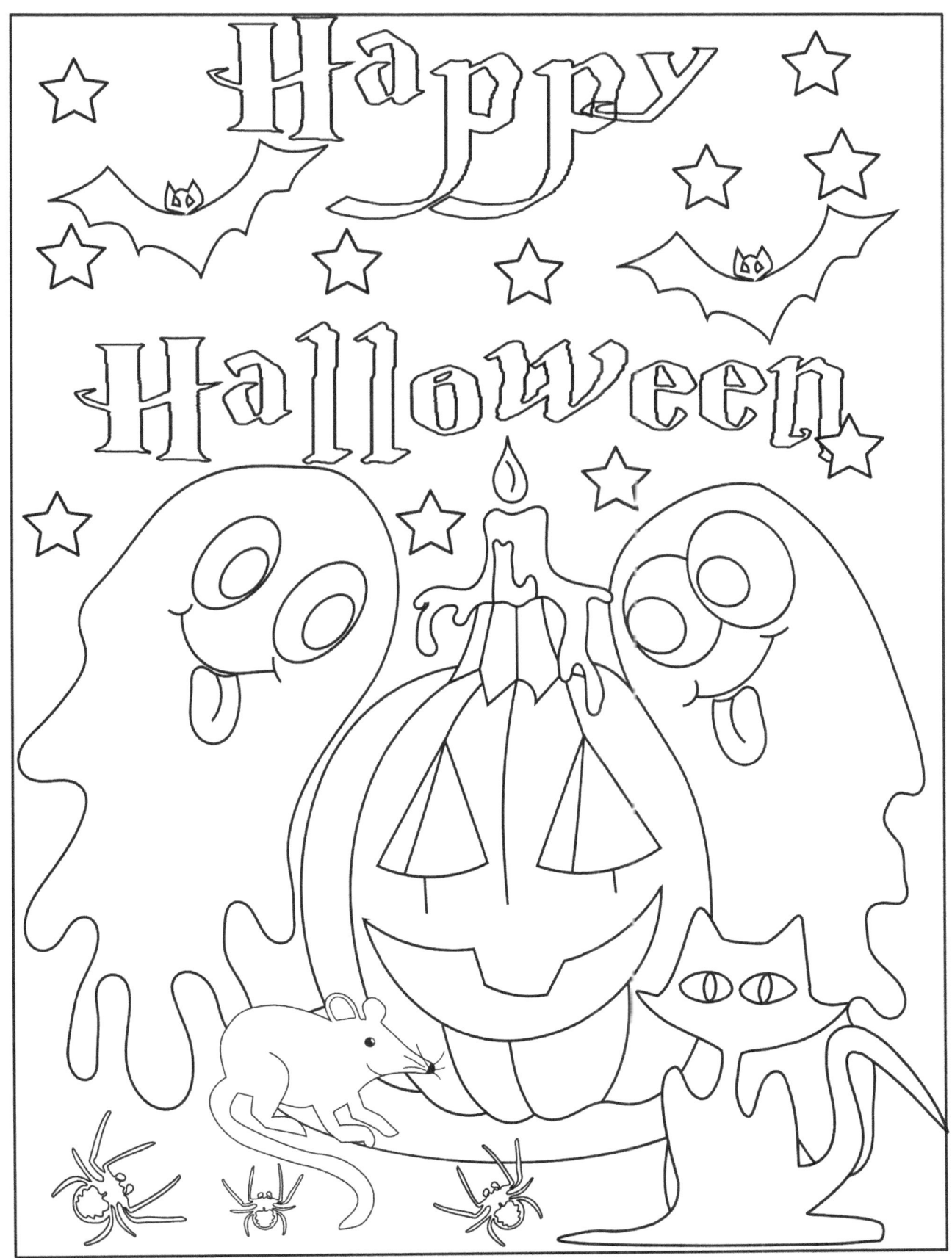

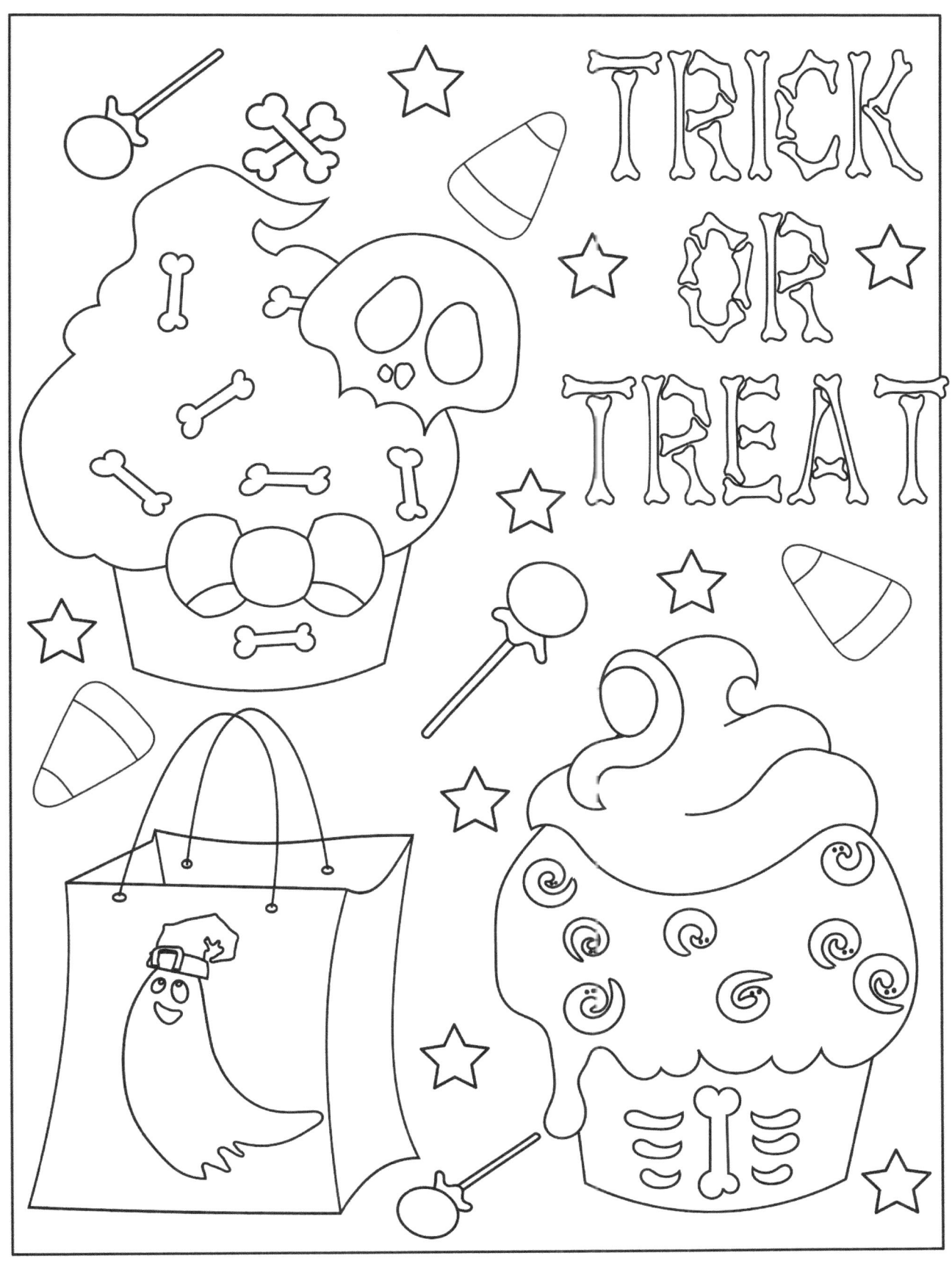

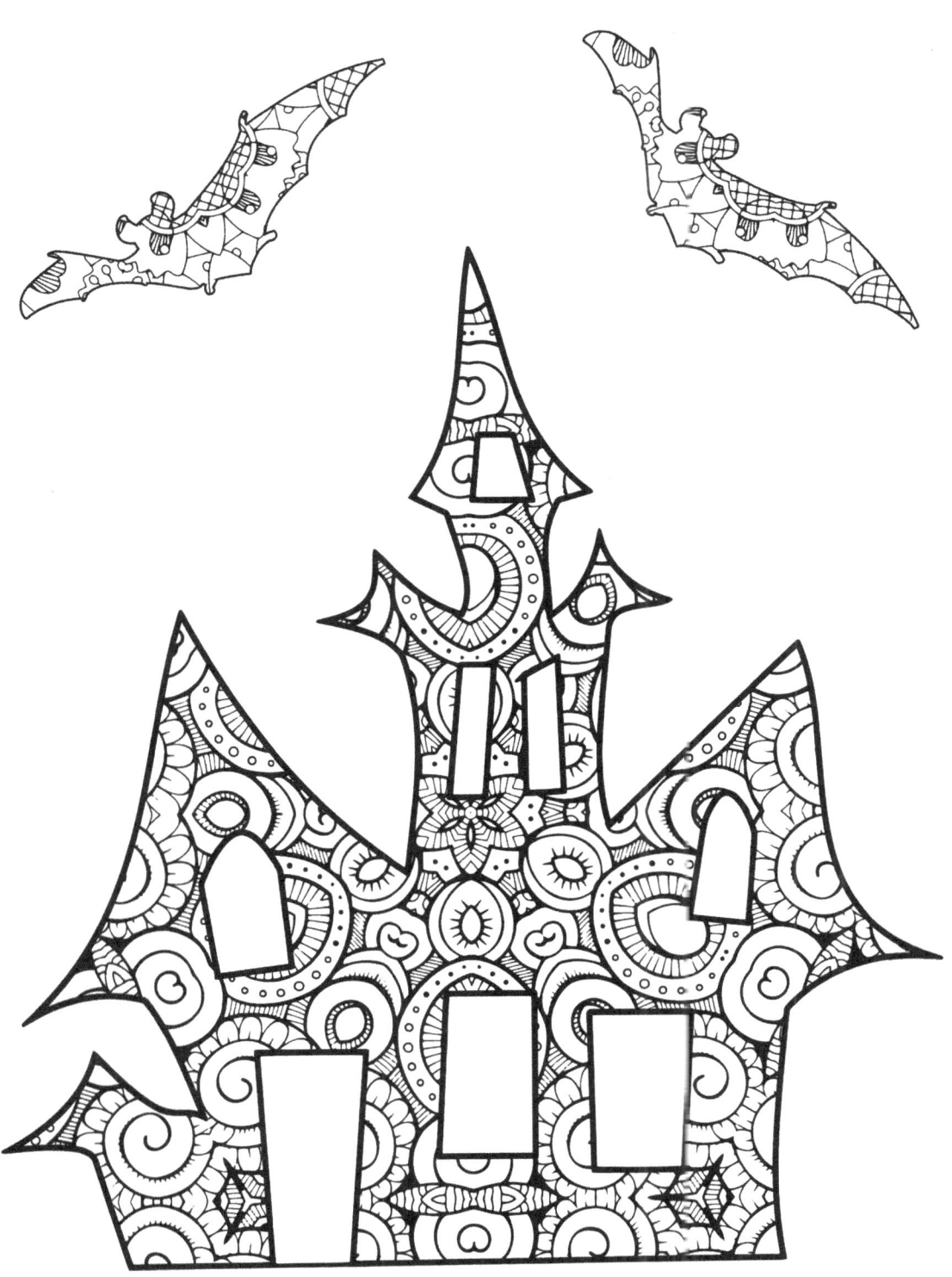

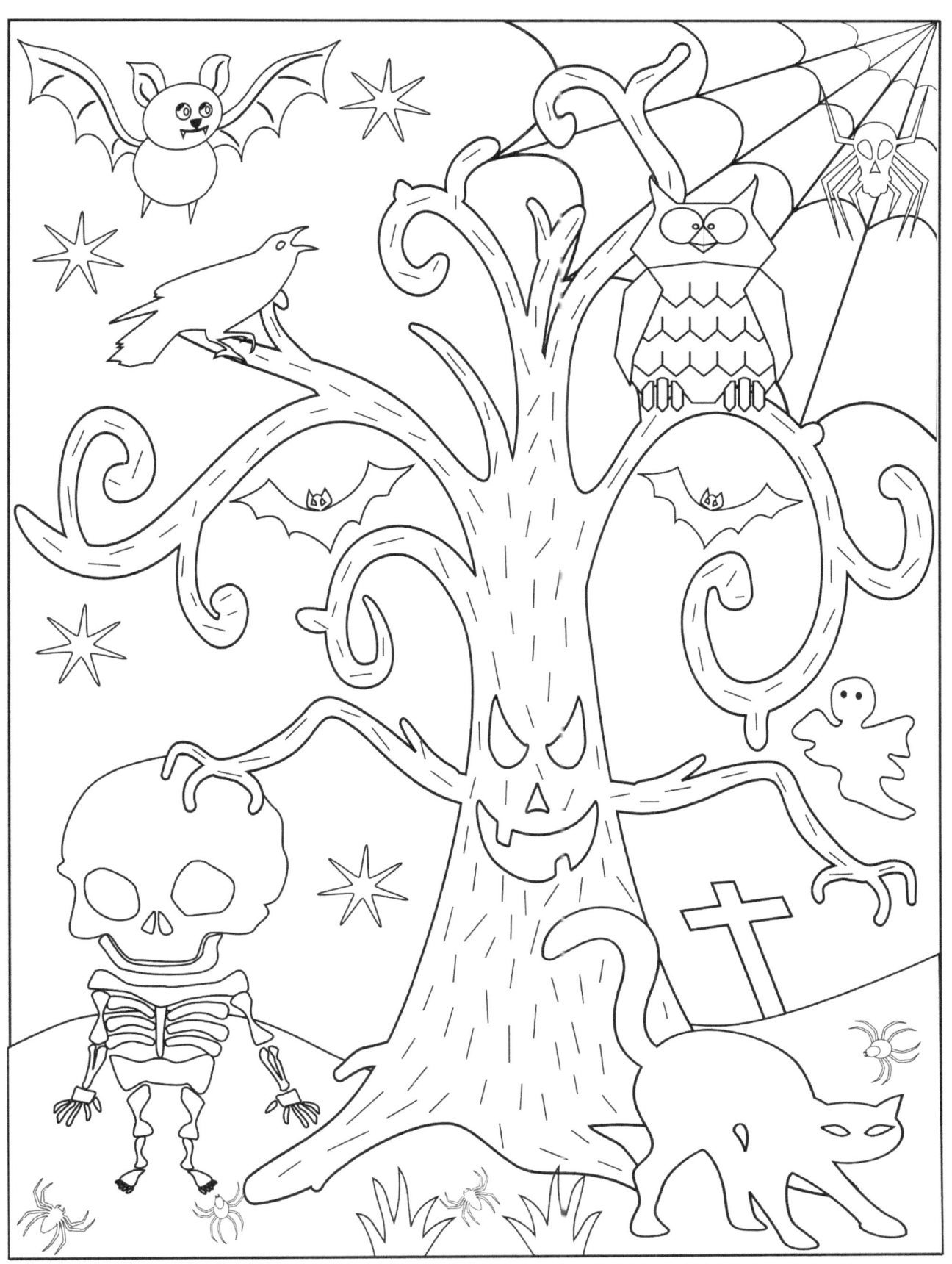

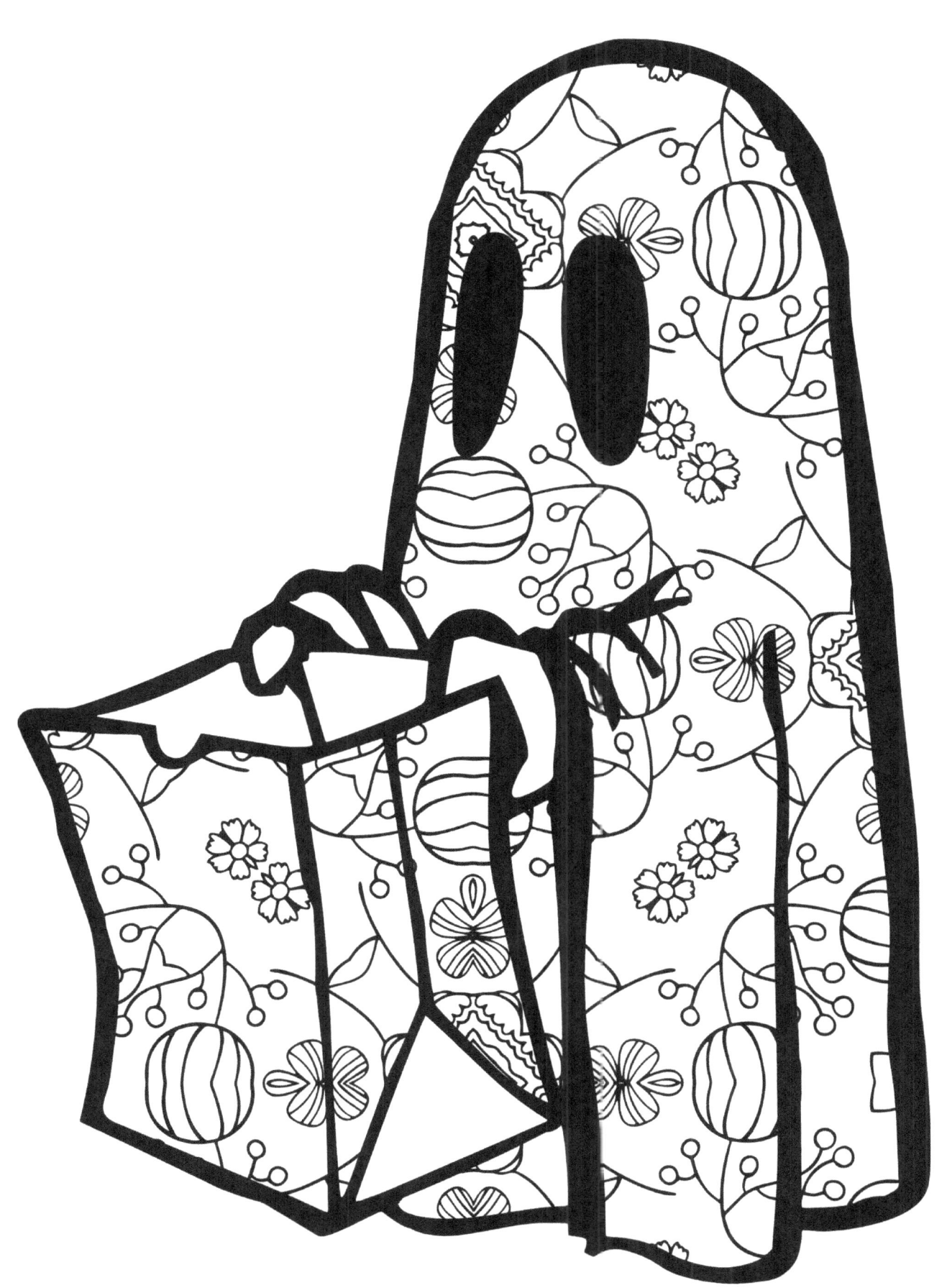

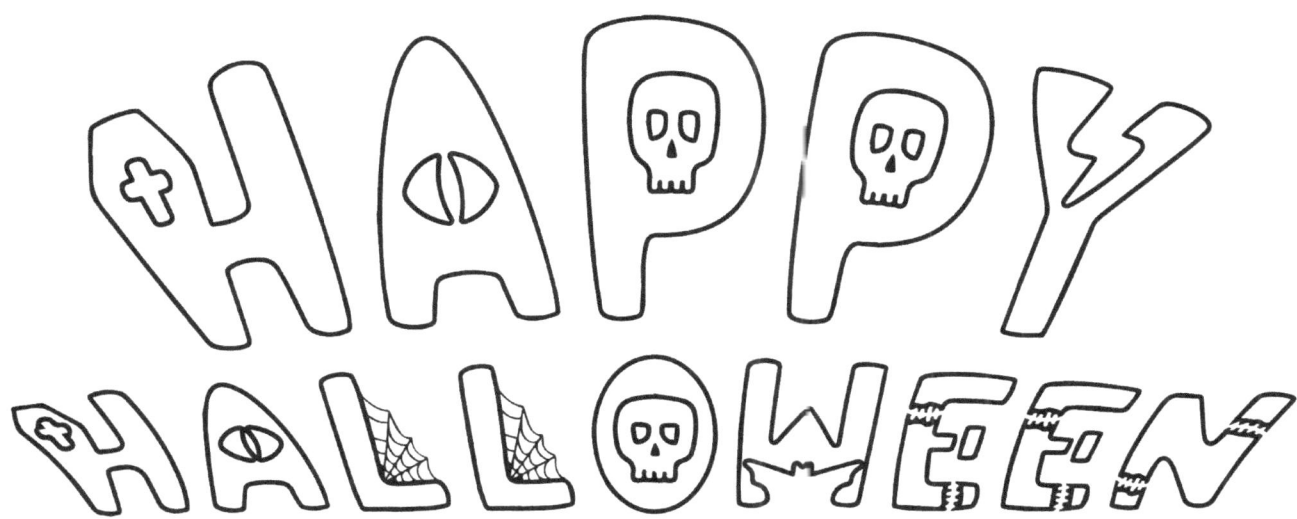

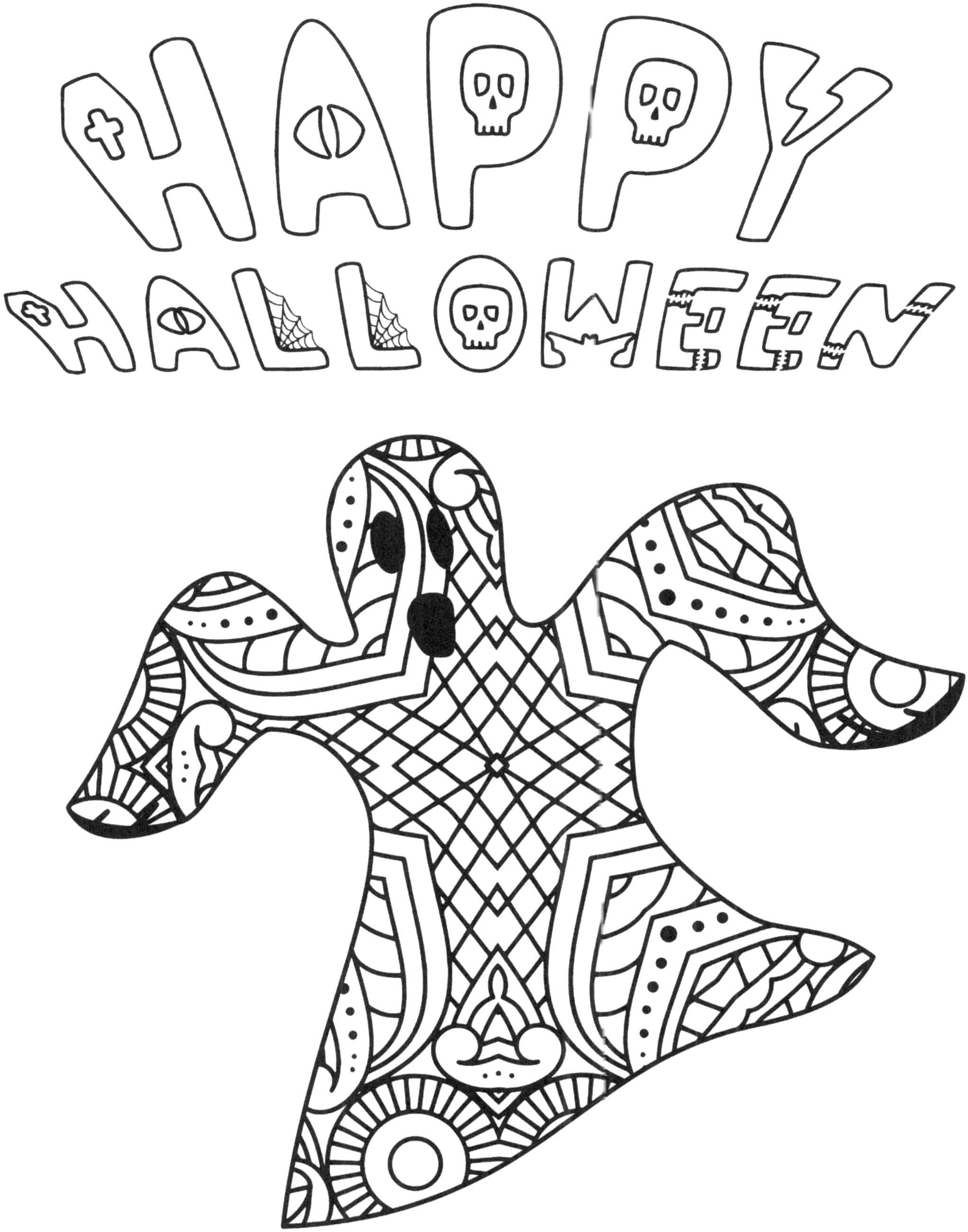

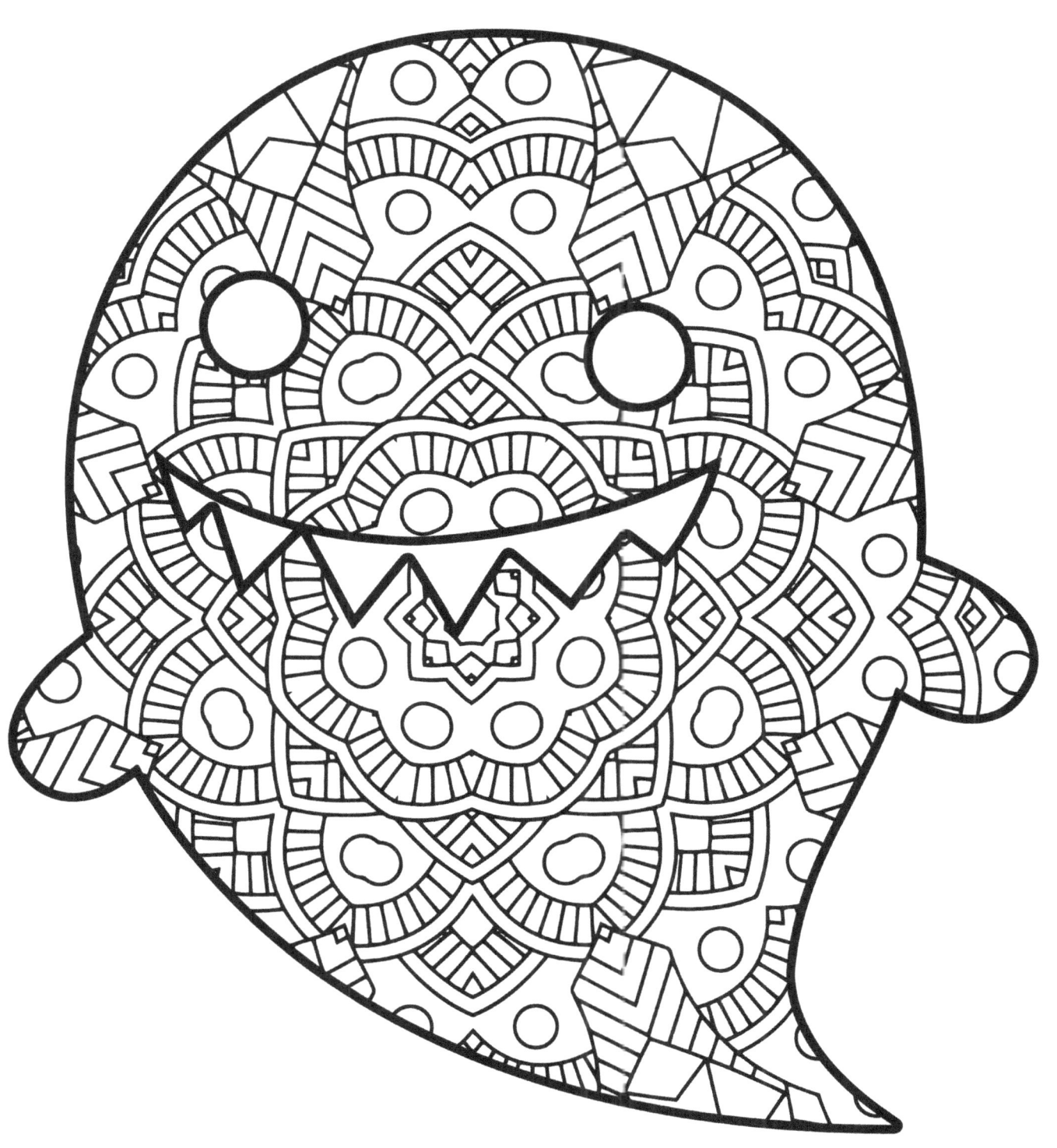

When black cats prowl
And pumpkins gleam,
May luck be yours
On Halloween

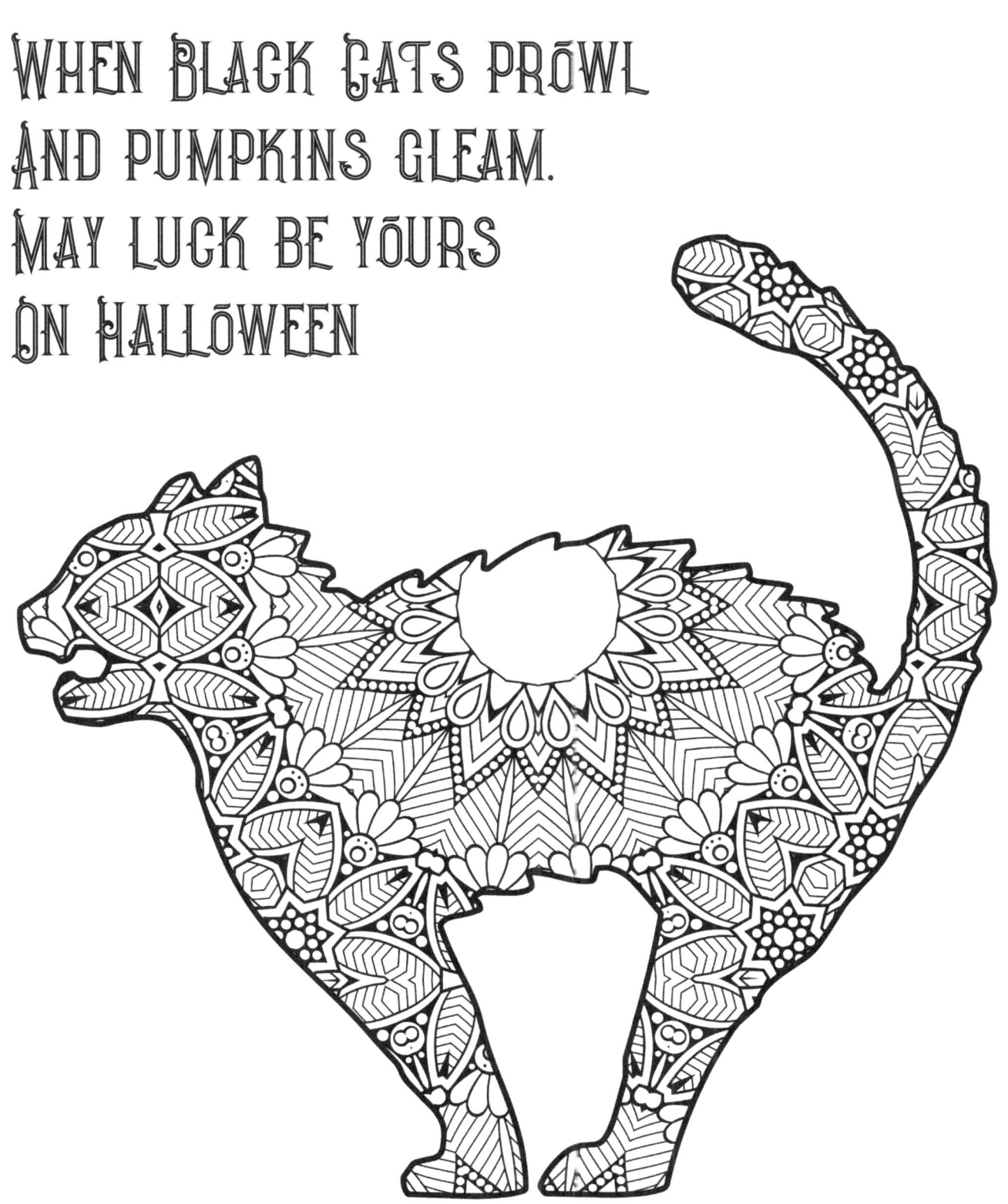

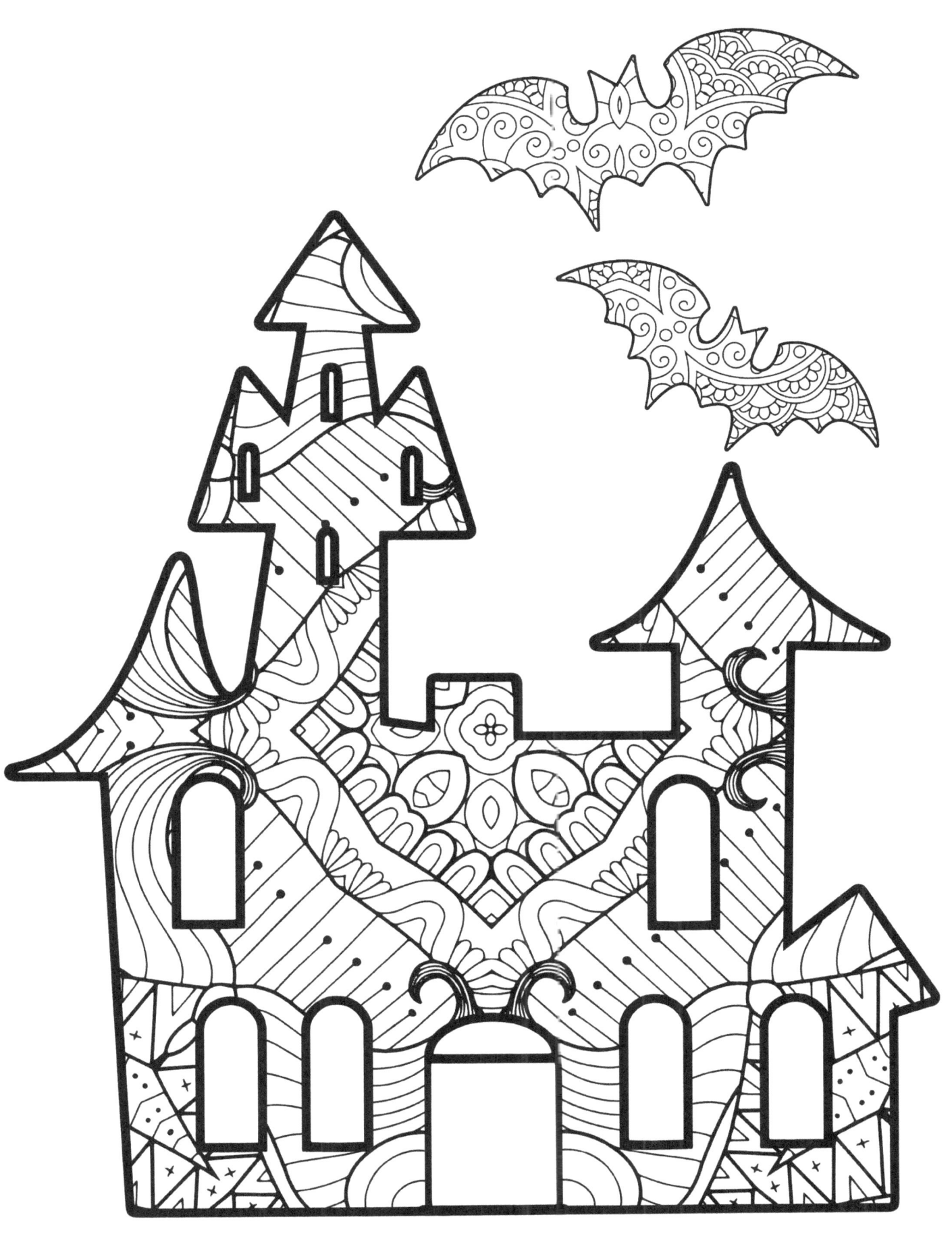

Trick or Treat
Bag of Sweets
Ghosts are Walking
Down the Street

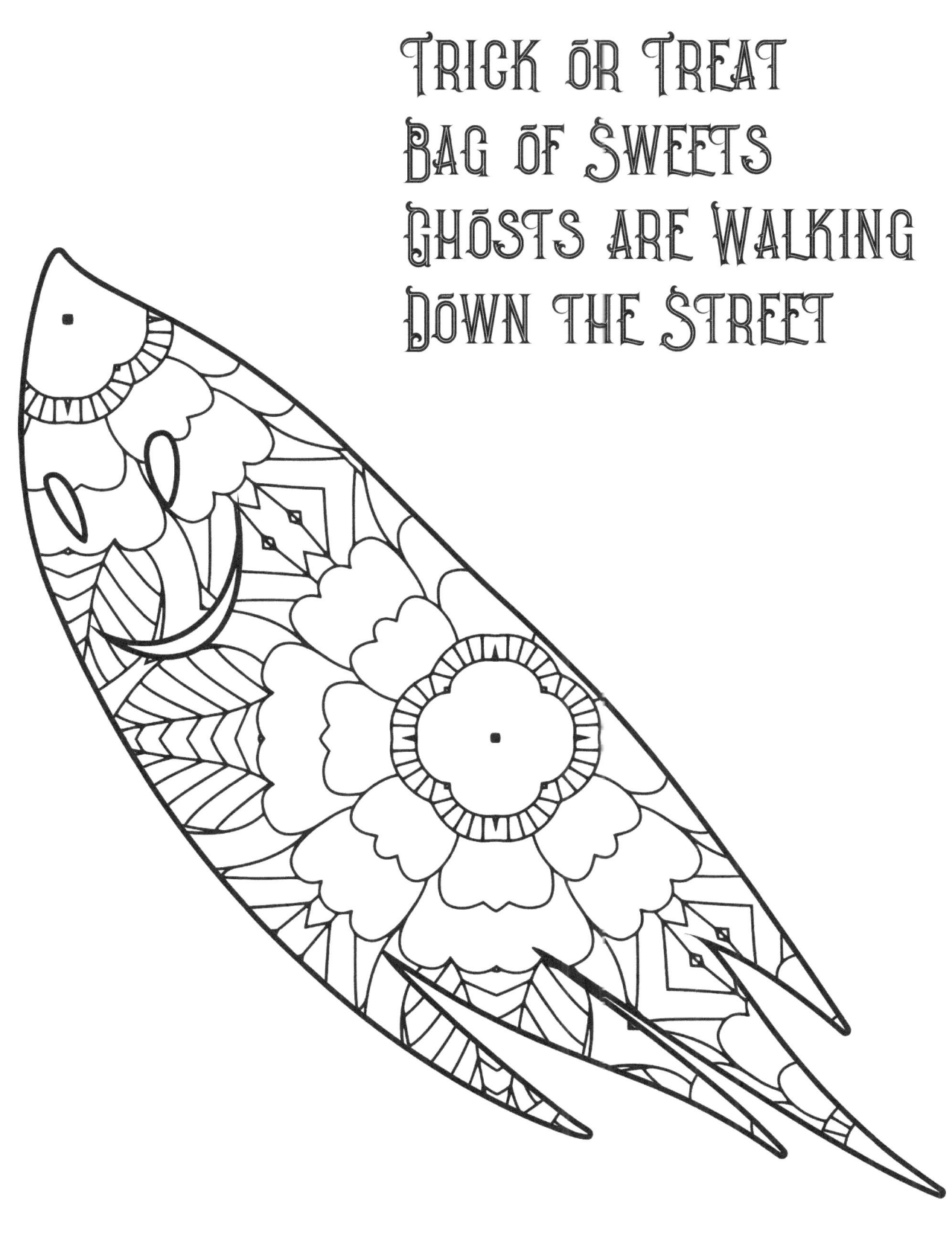

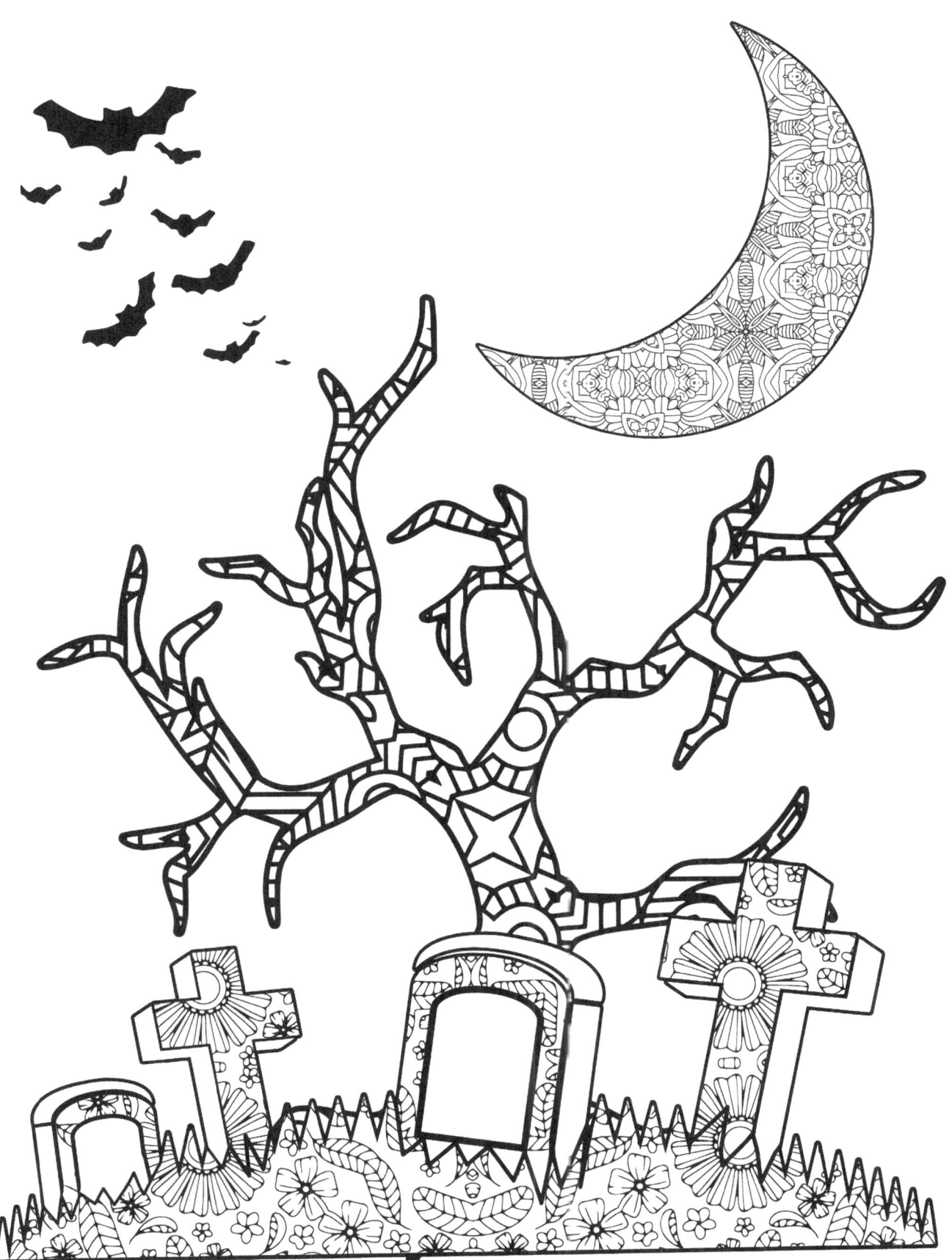

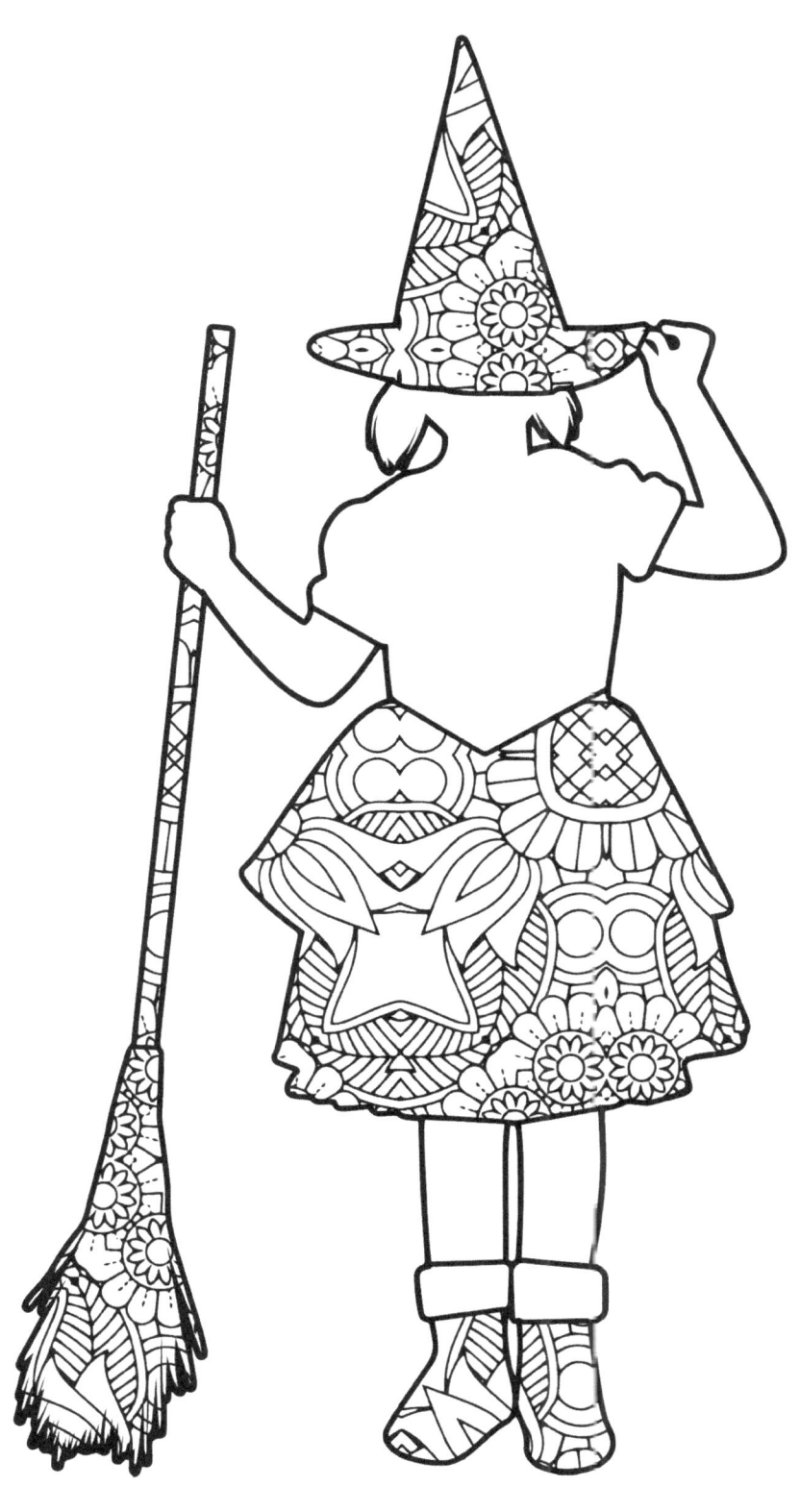

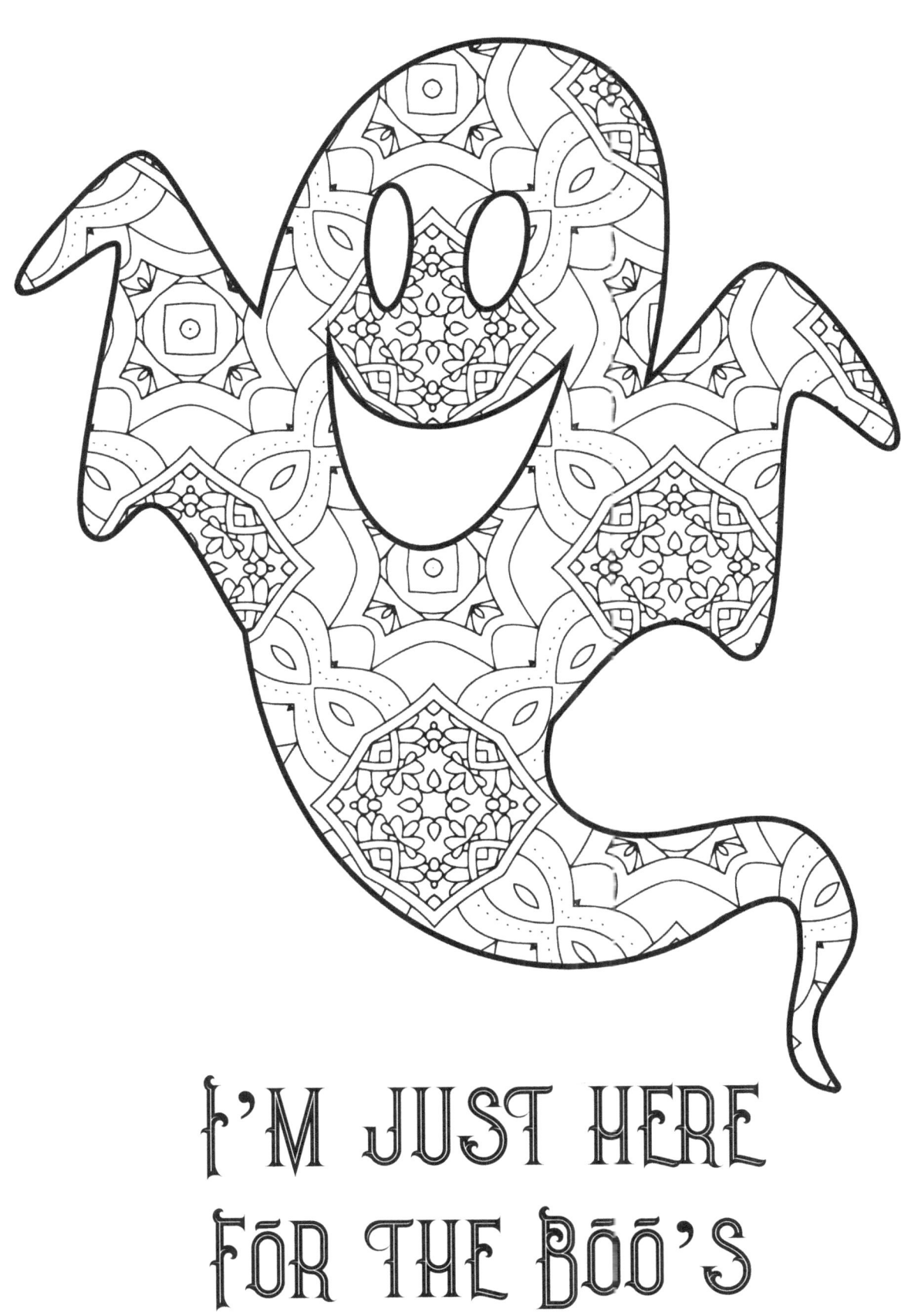

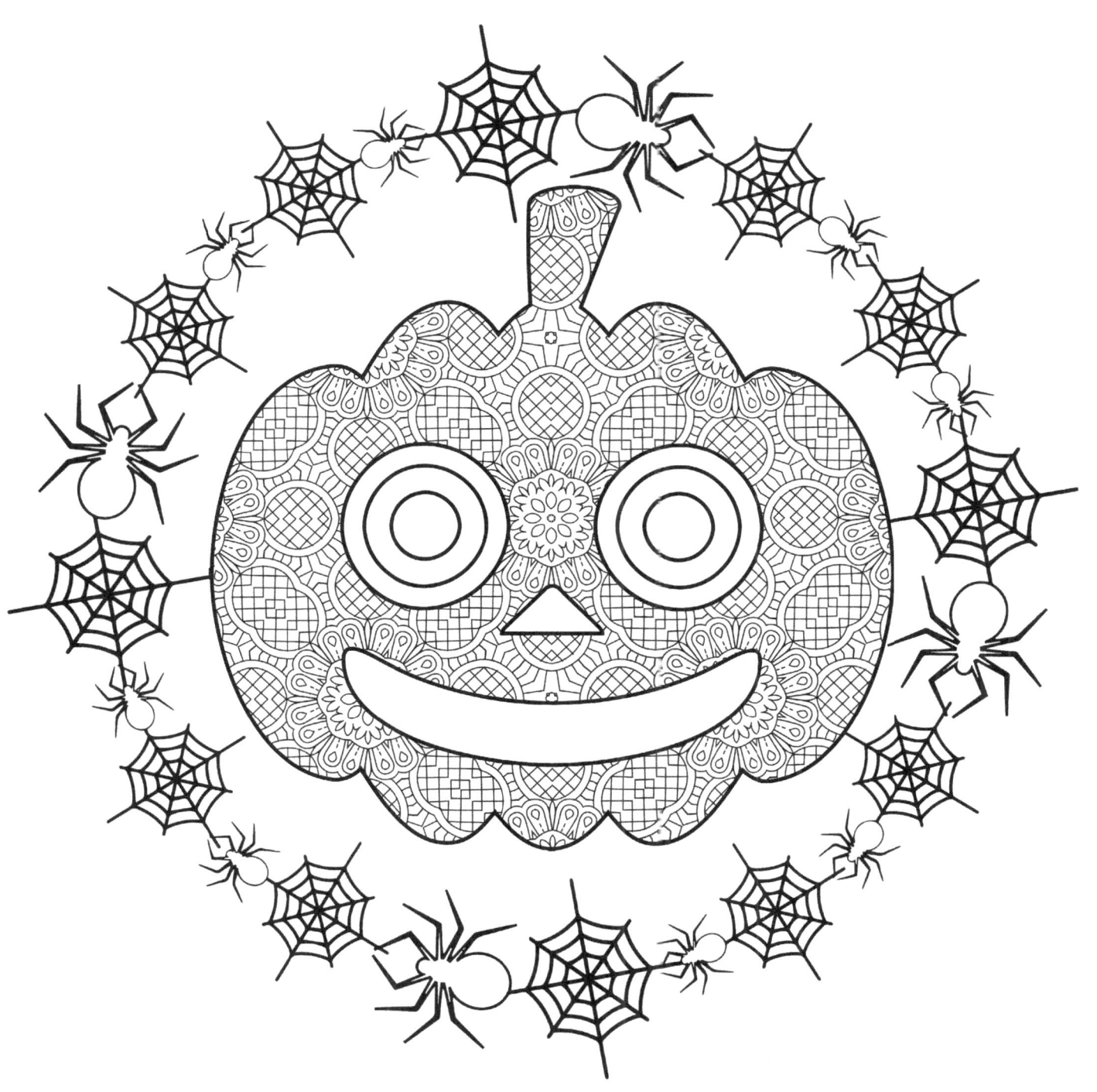

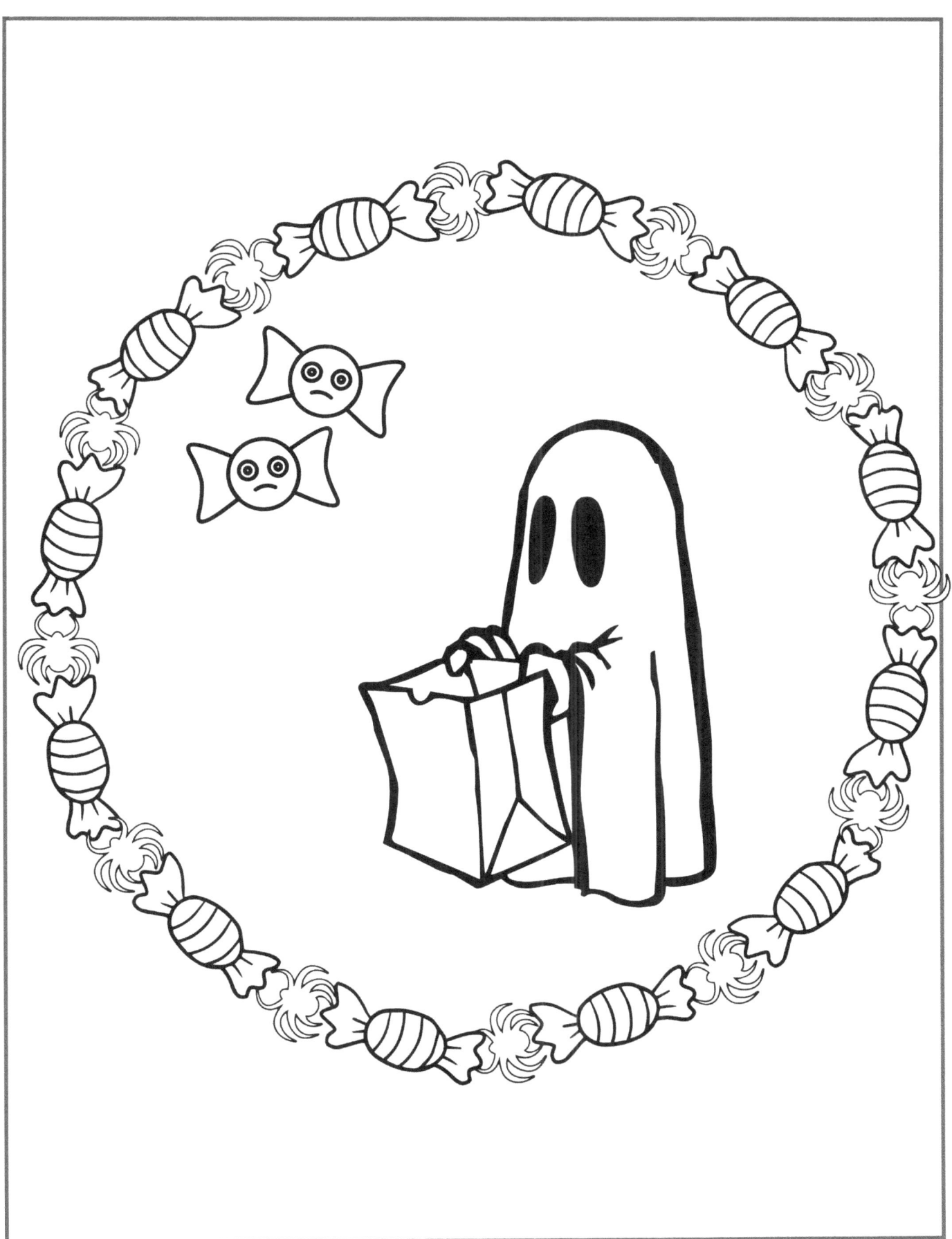

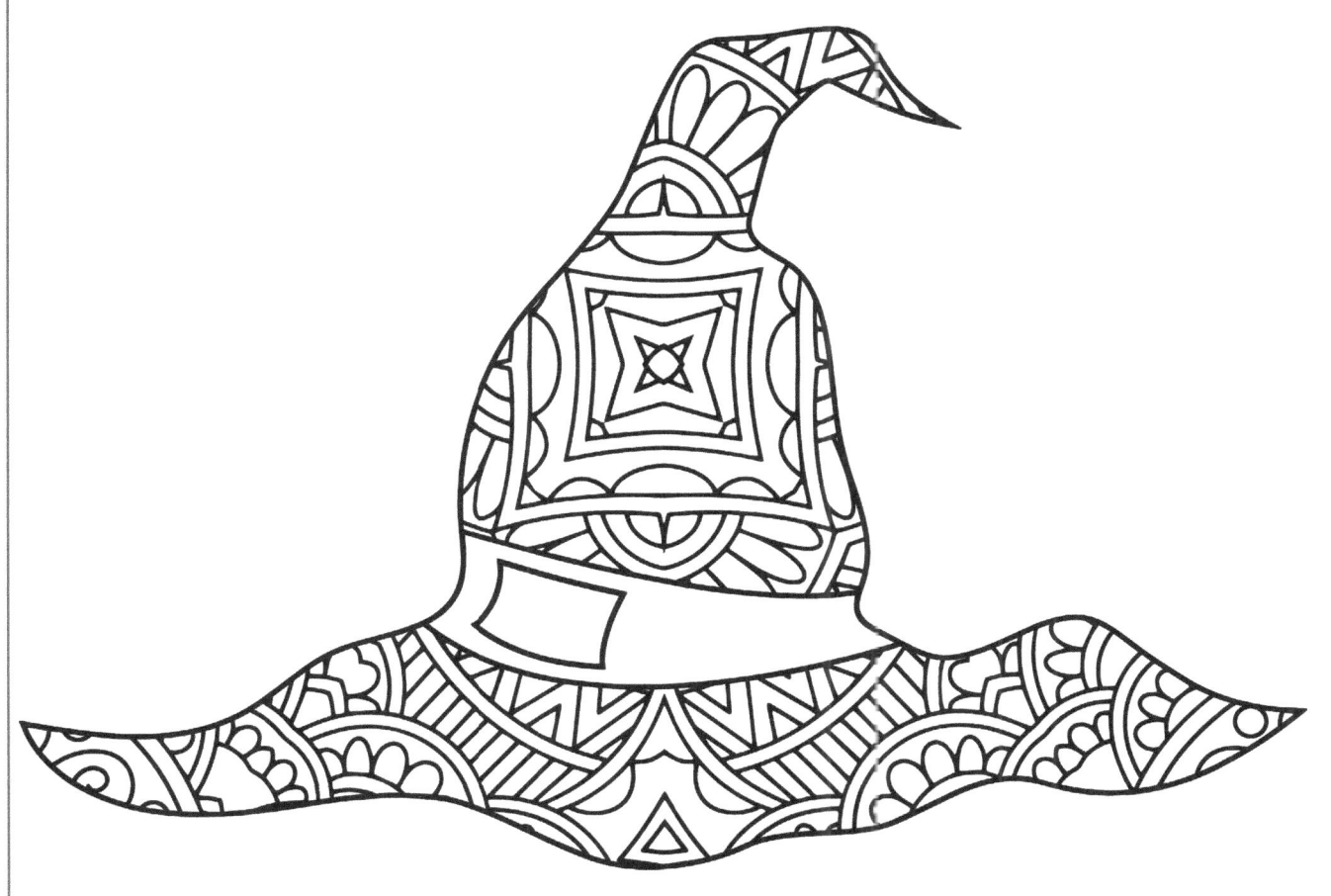

You say witch like it's a bad thing!

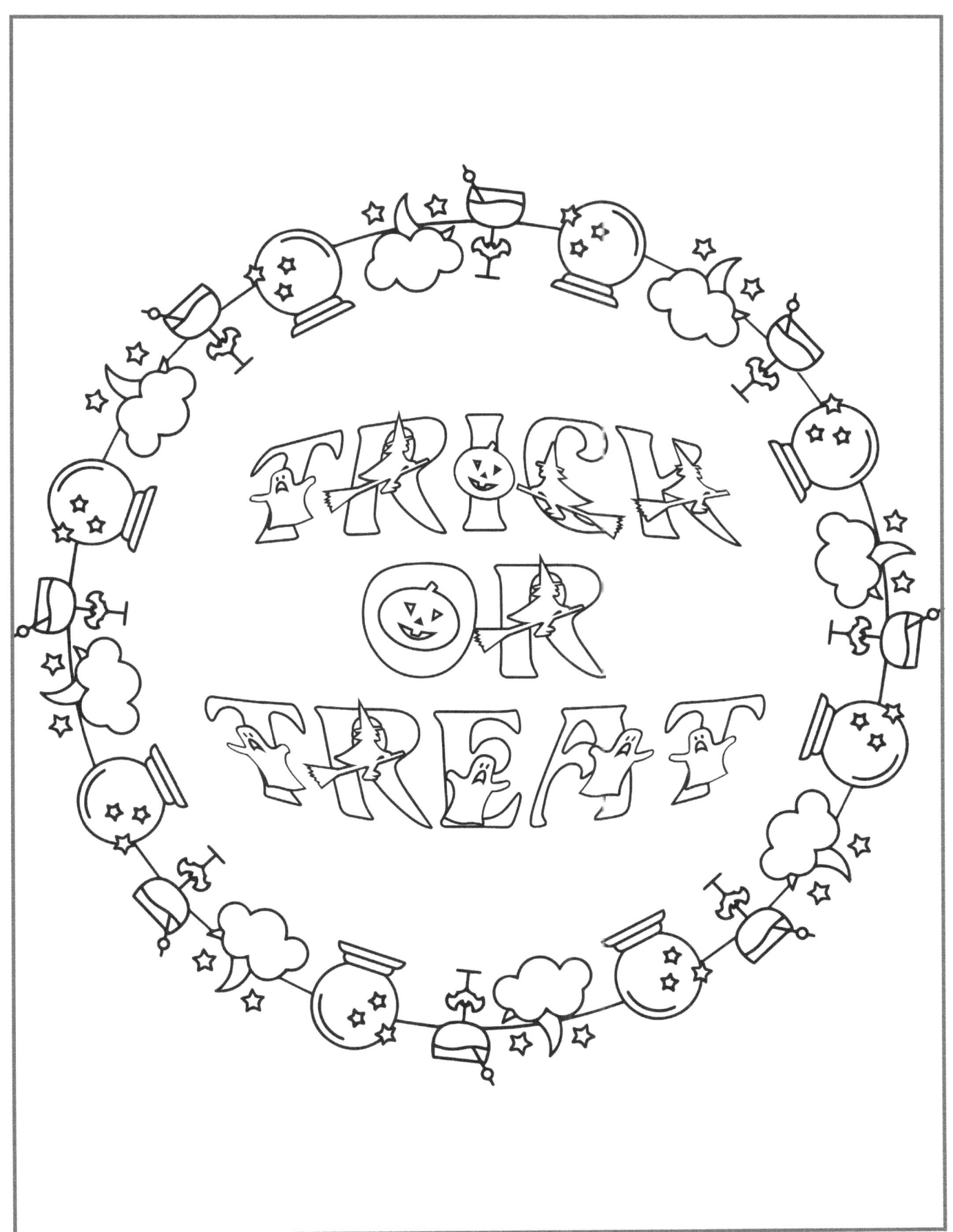

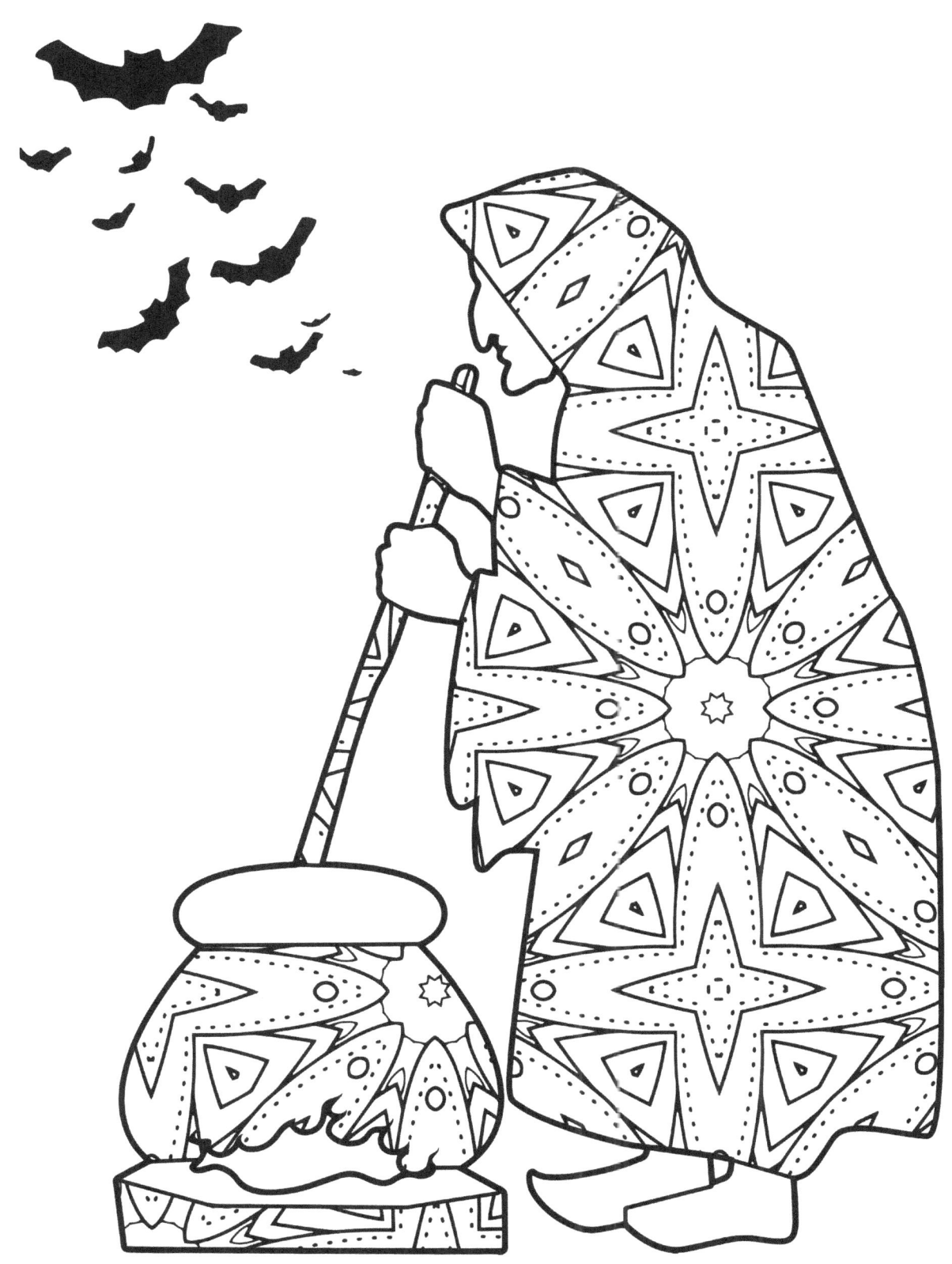

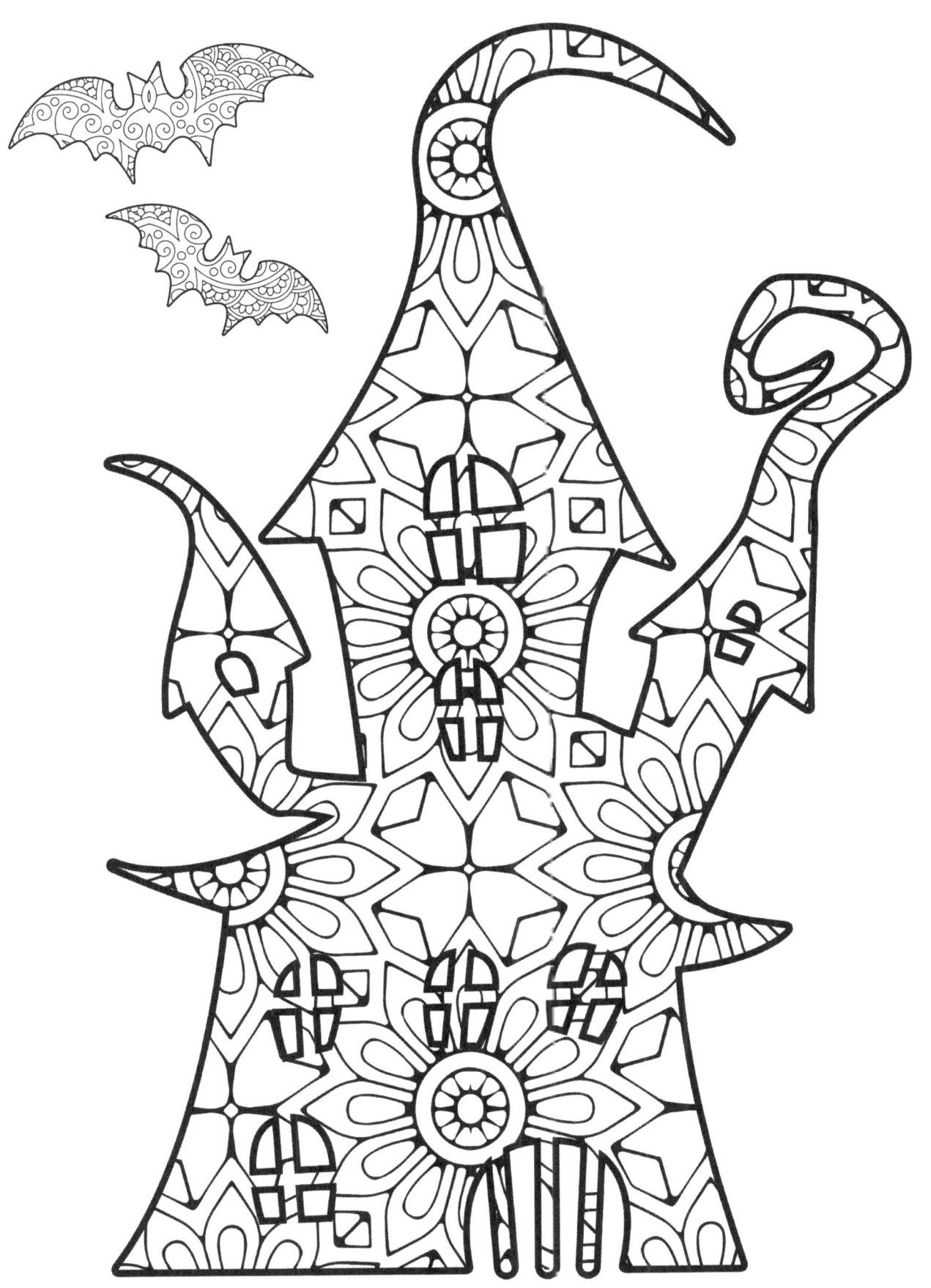

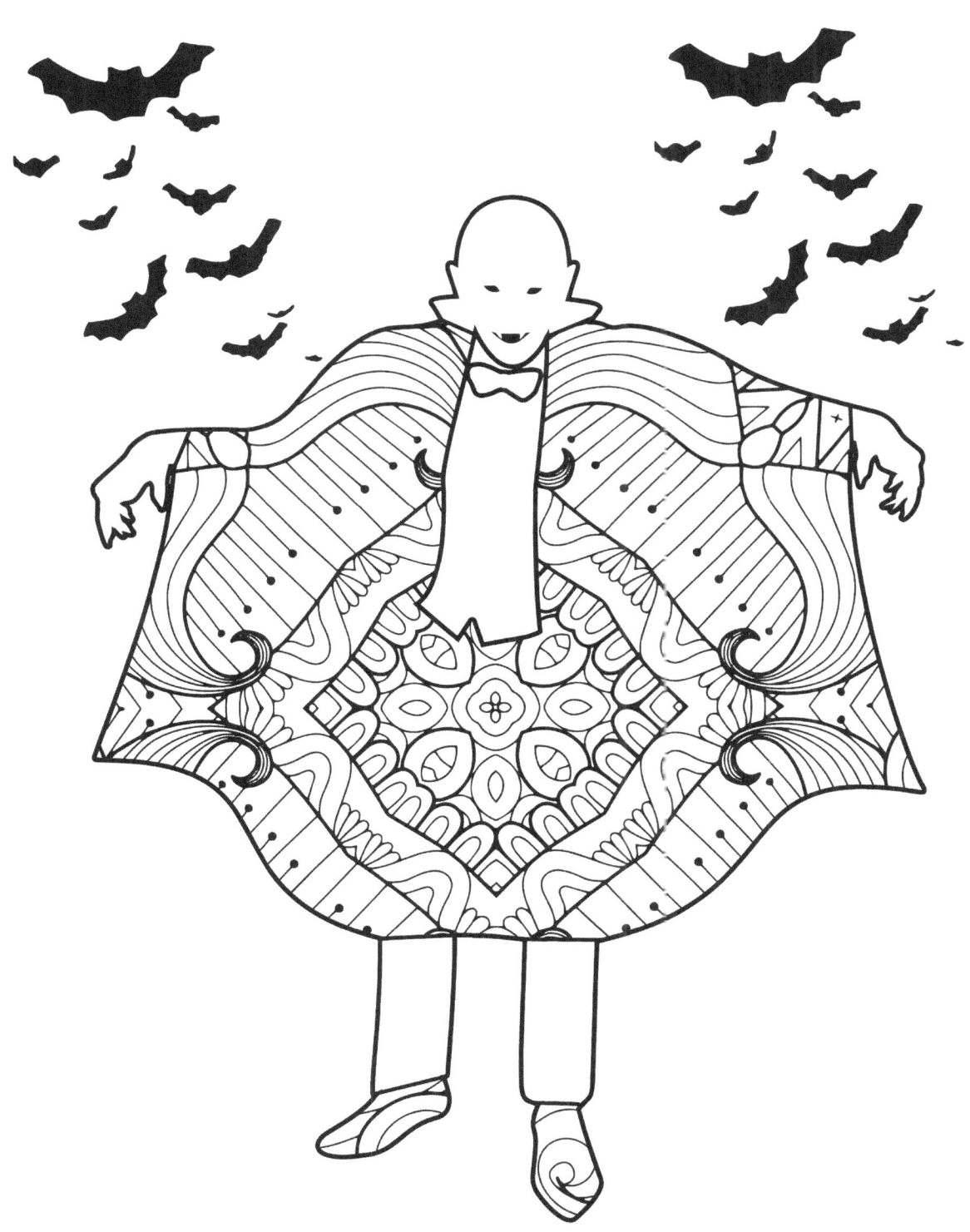

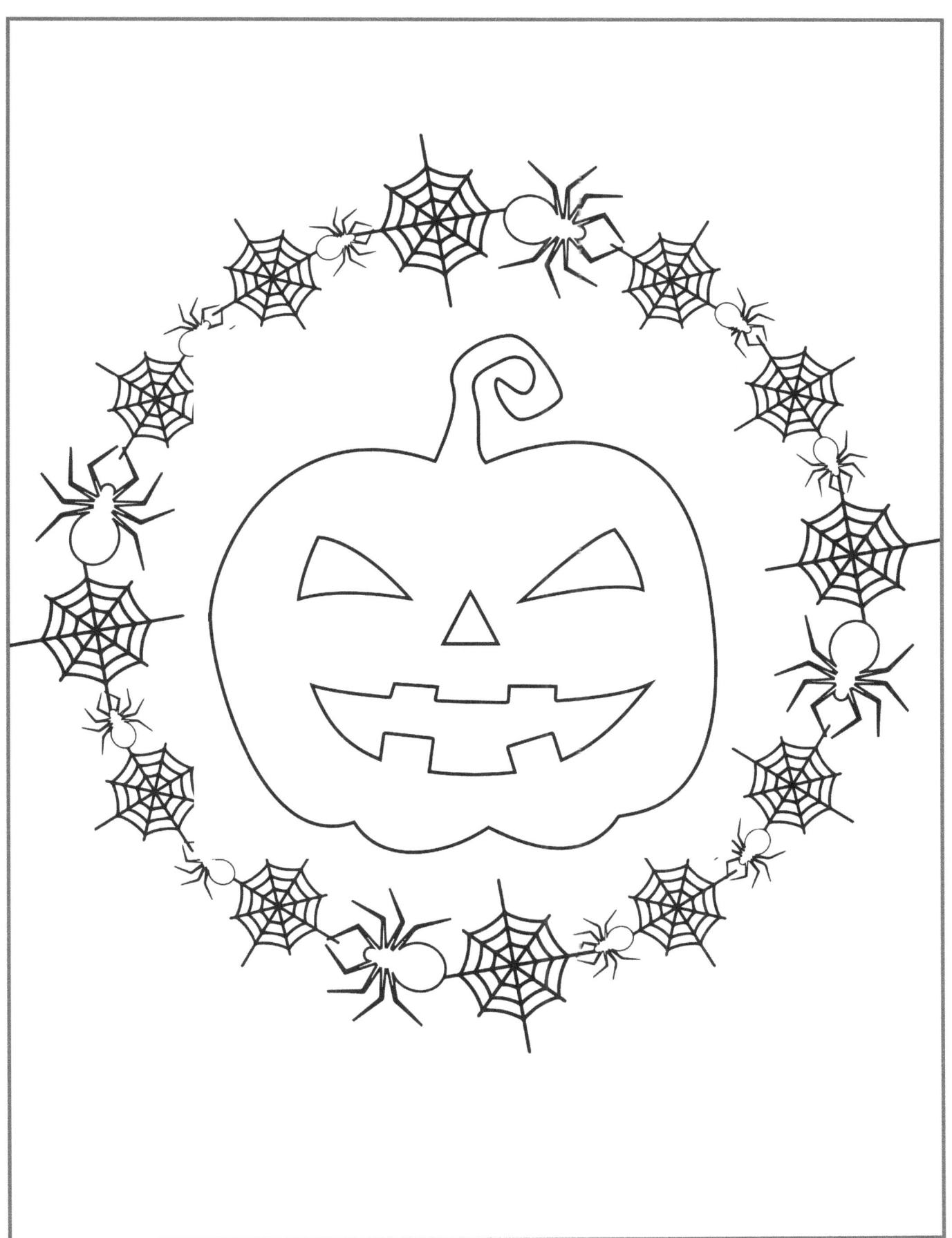

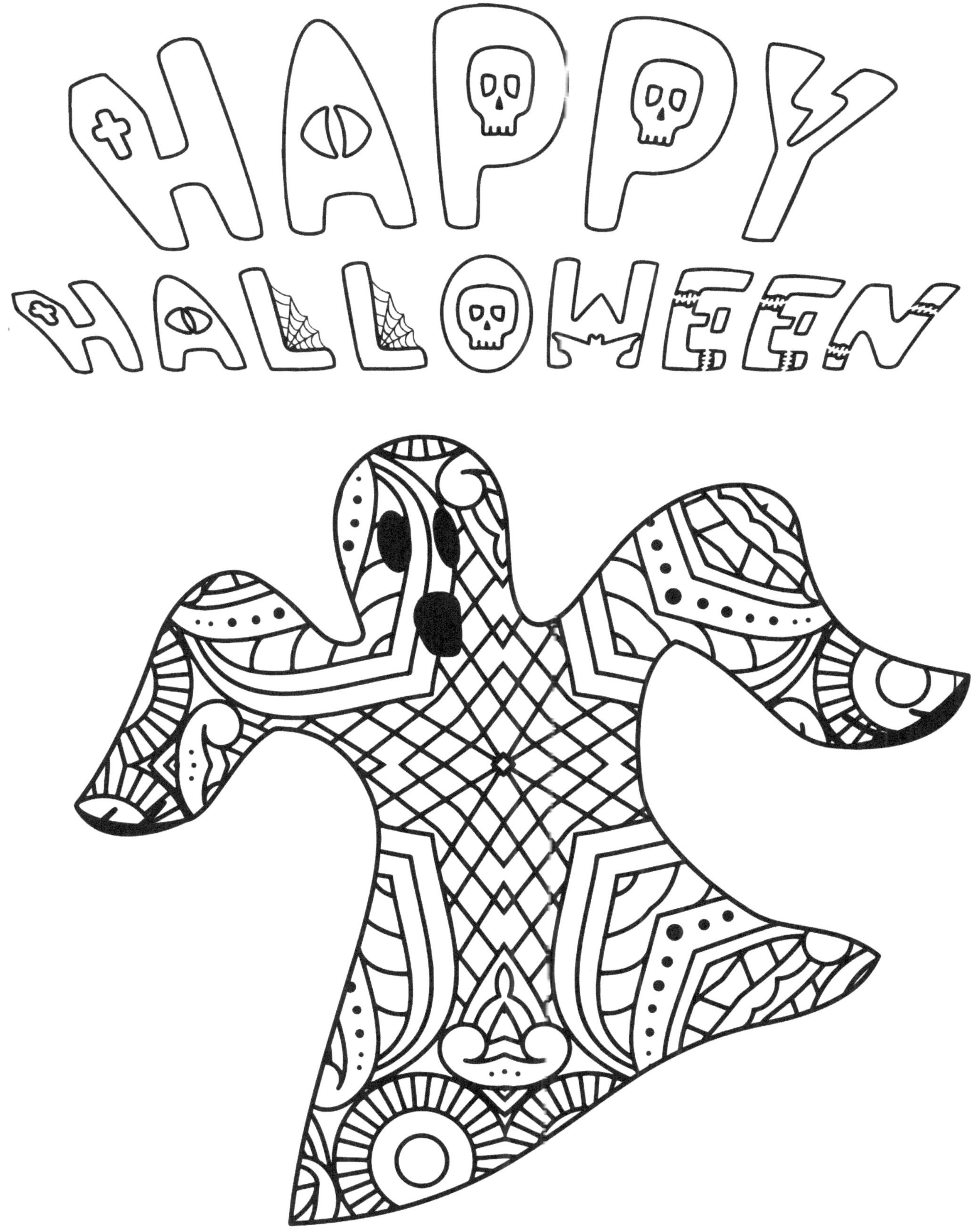

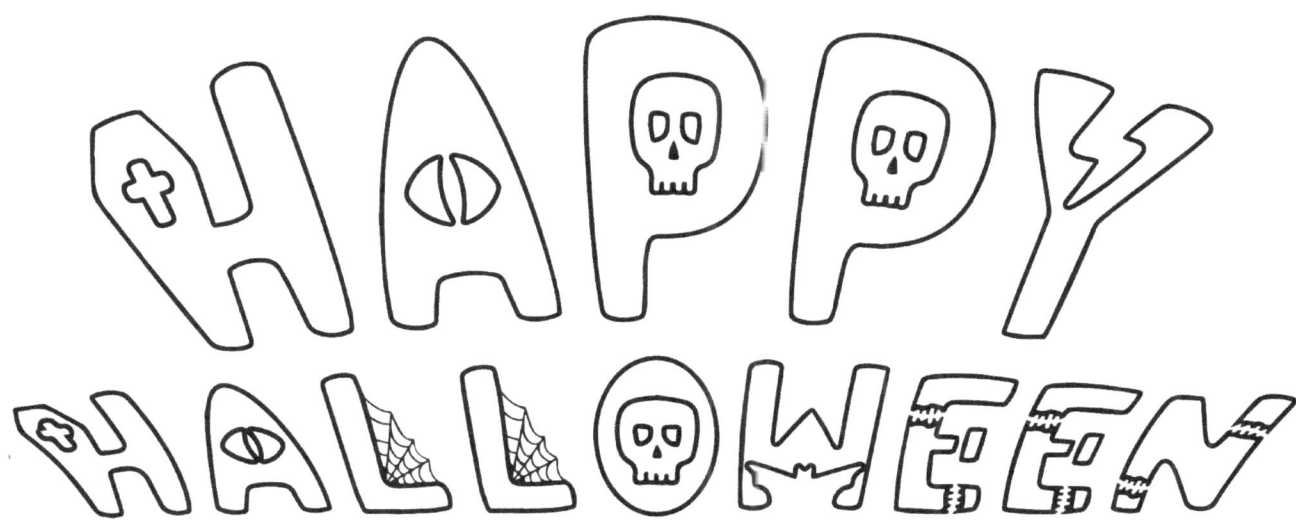

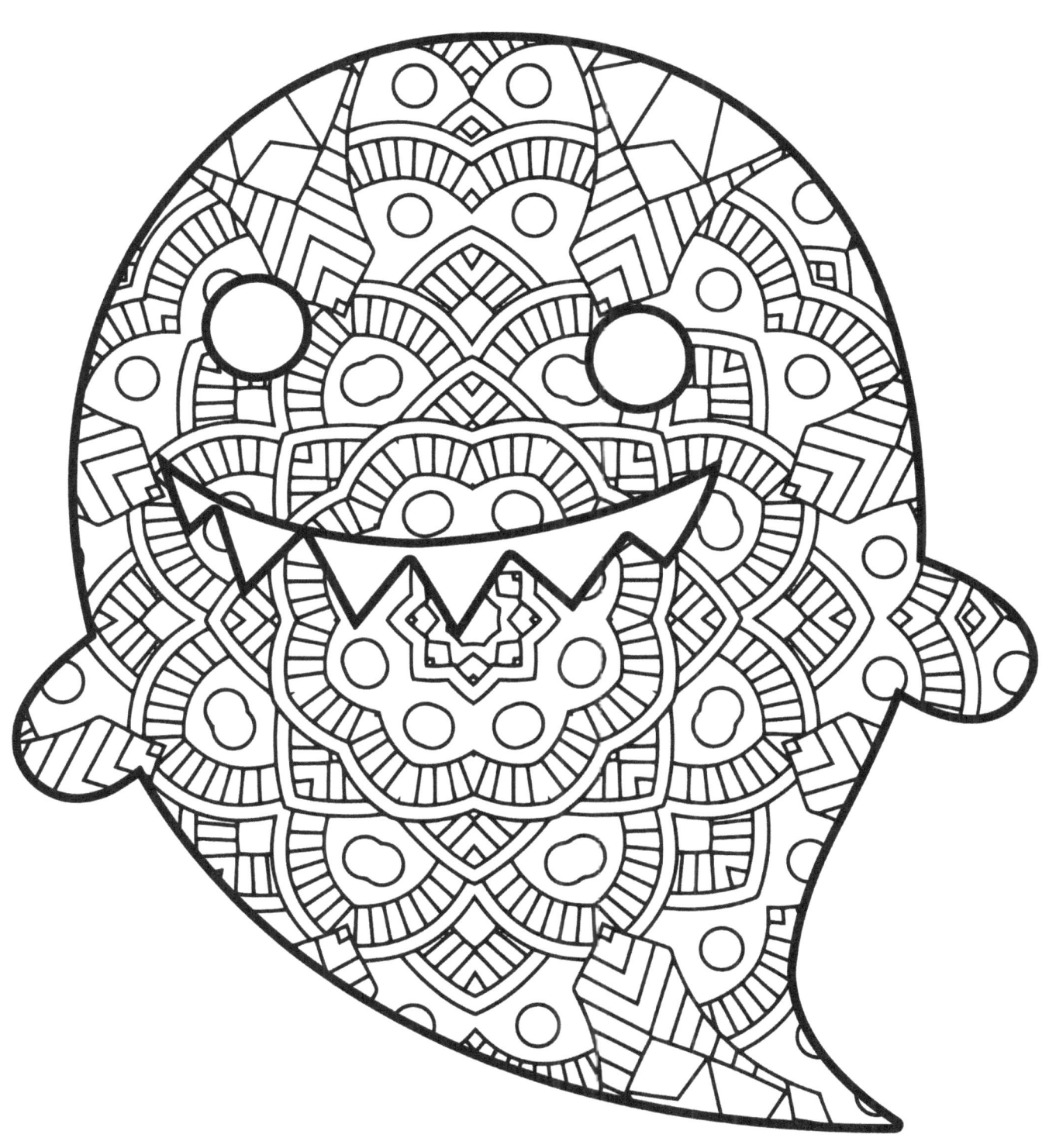

When black cats prowl
And pumpkins gleam.
May luck be yours
On Halloween

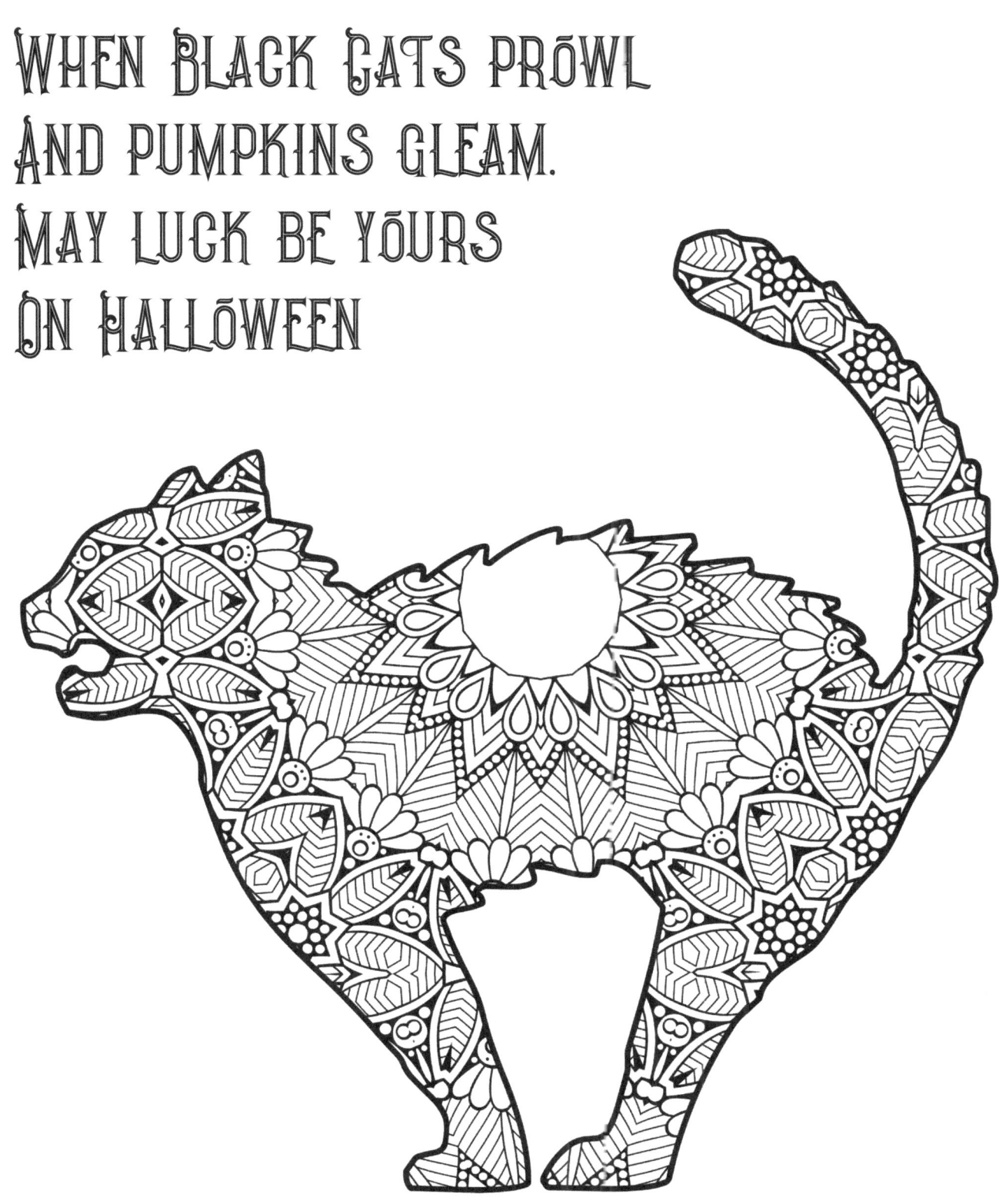

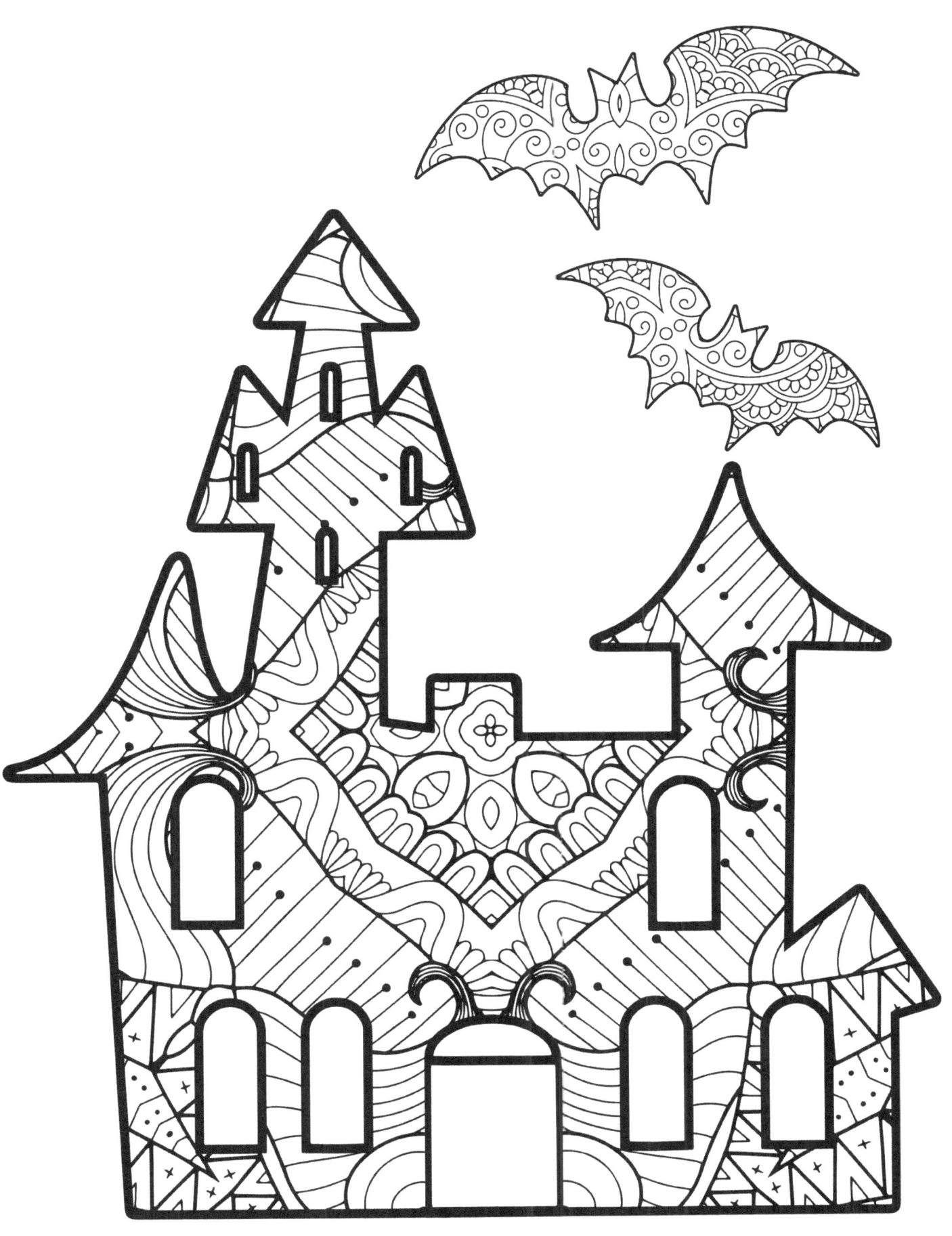

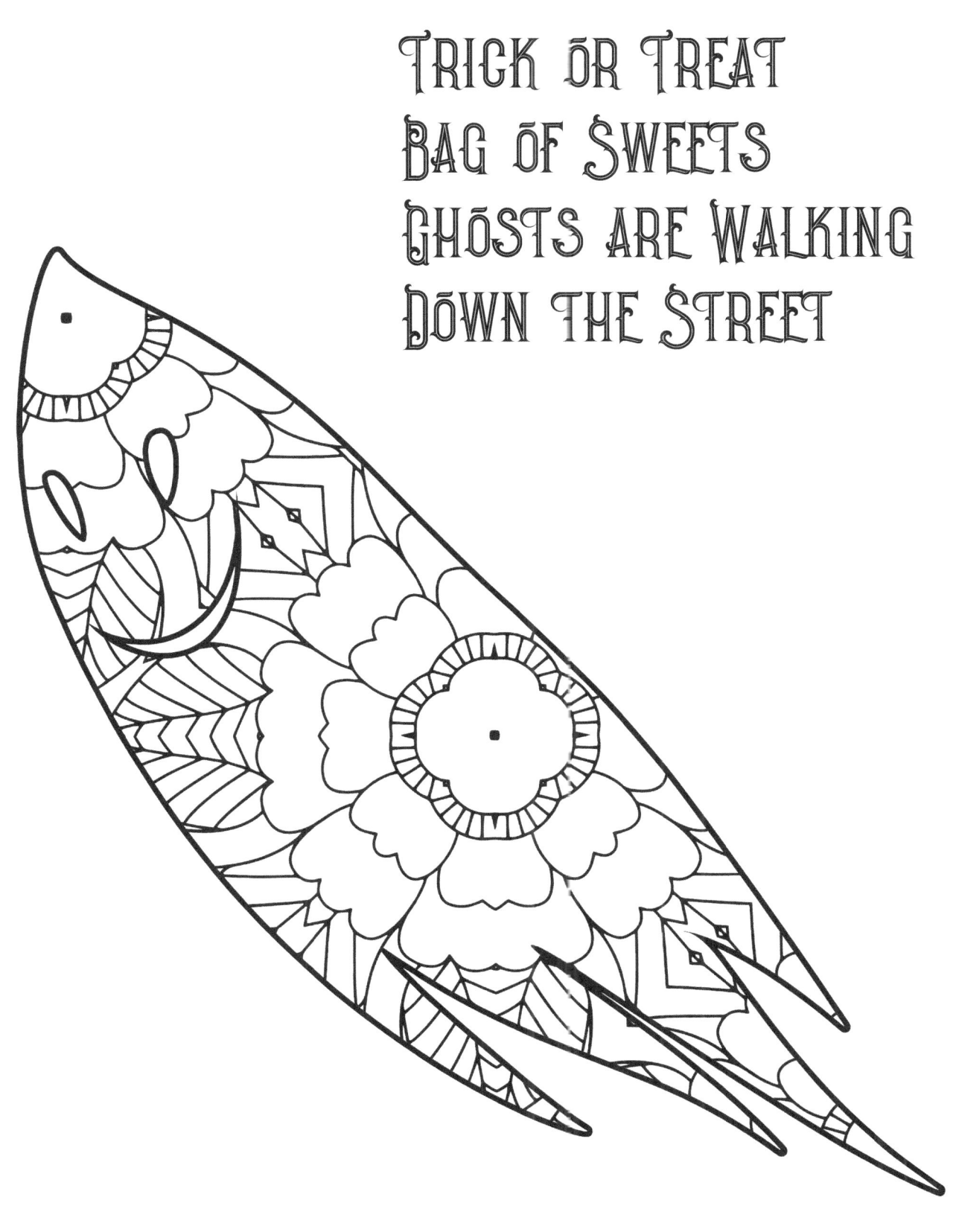

Trick or Treat
Bag of Sweets
Ghosts are Walking
Down the Street

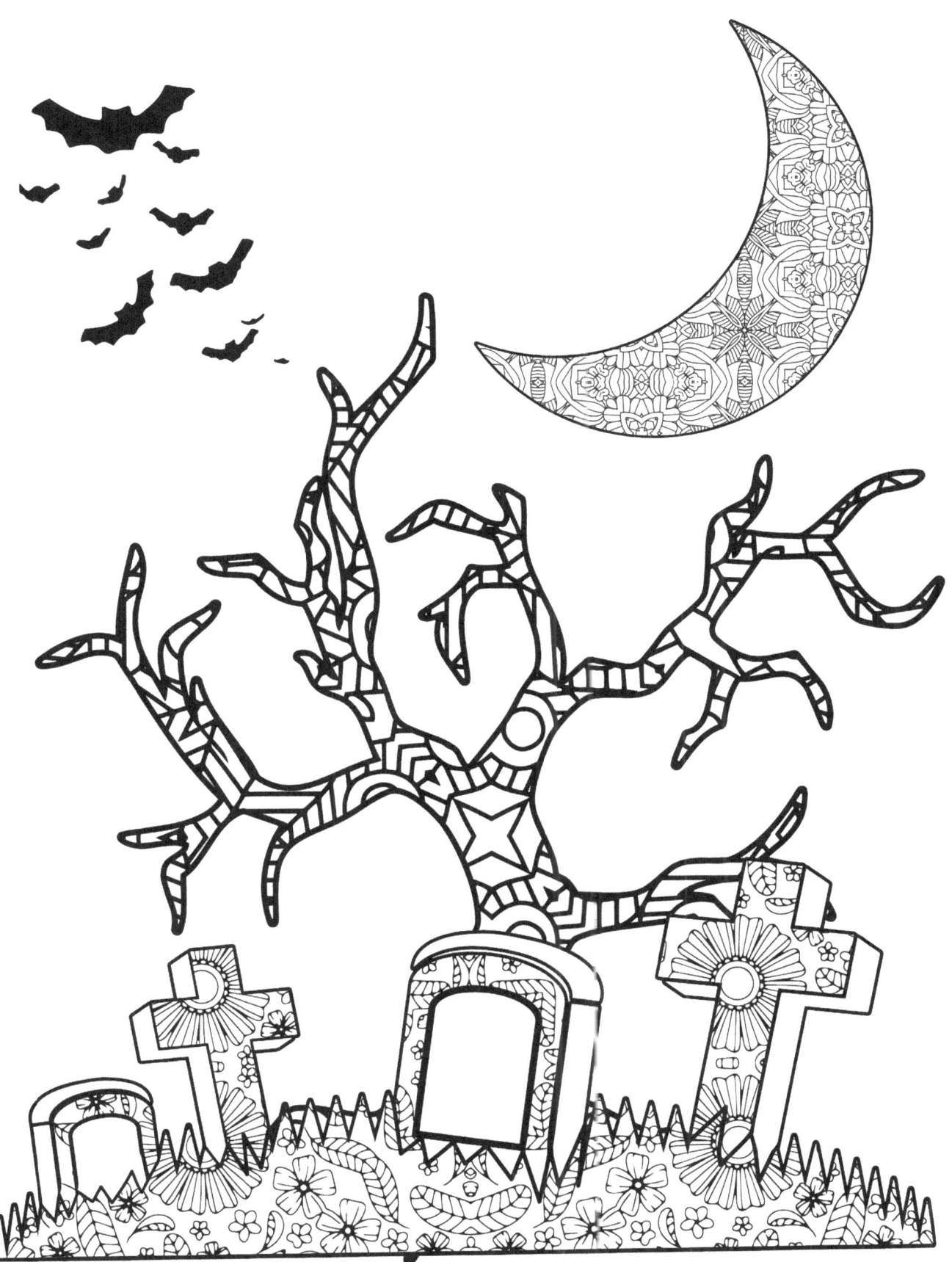

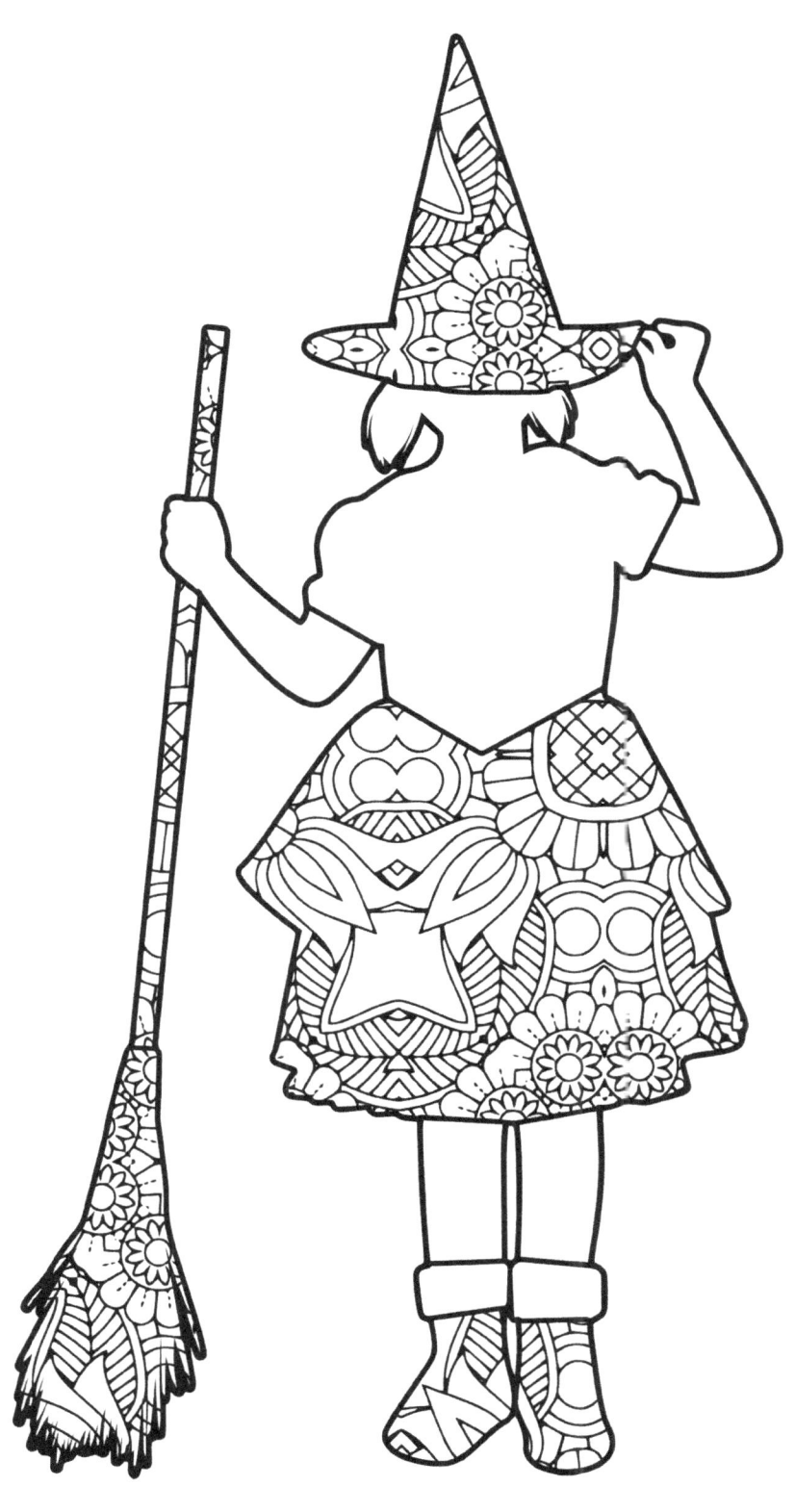

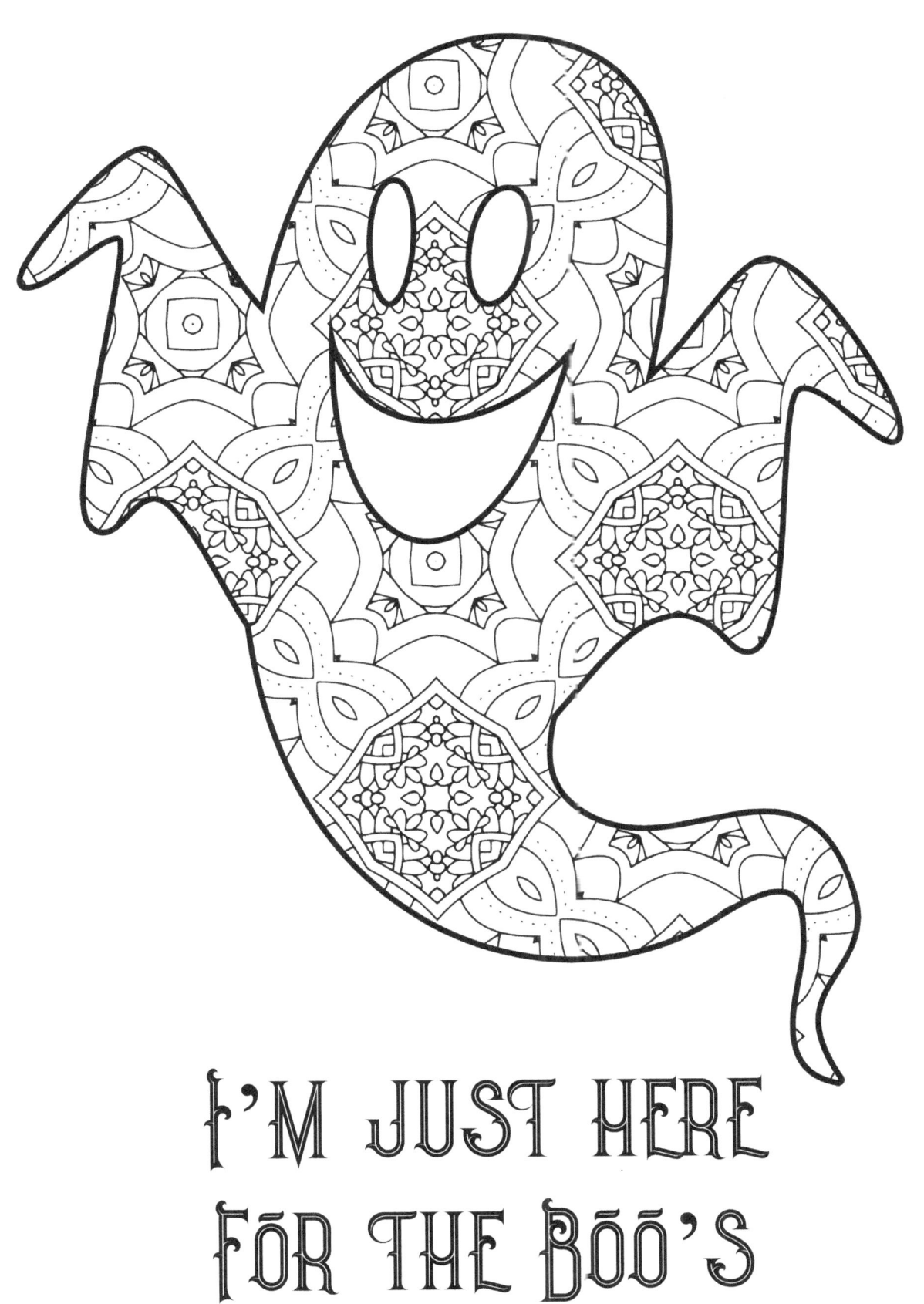

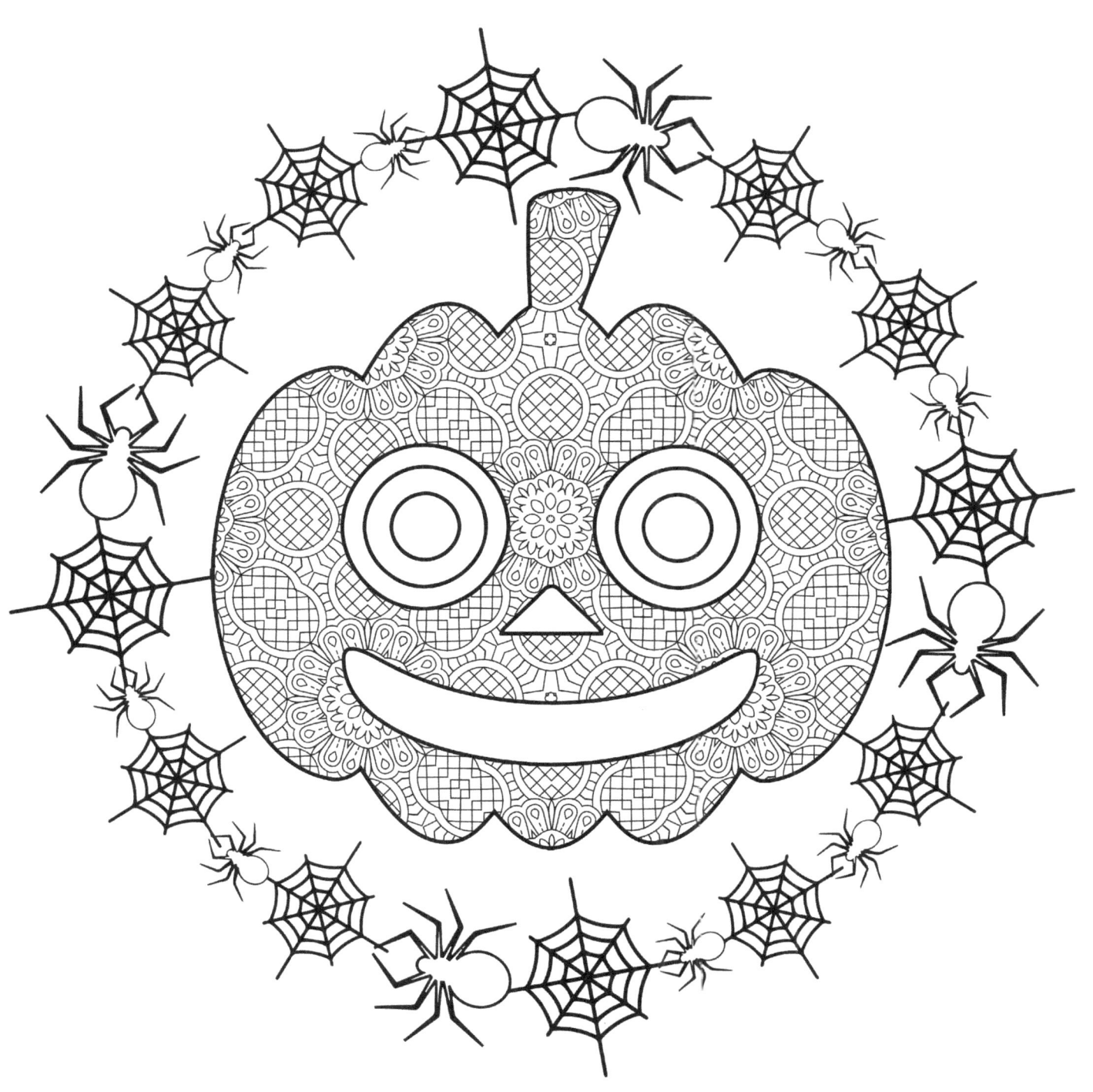

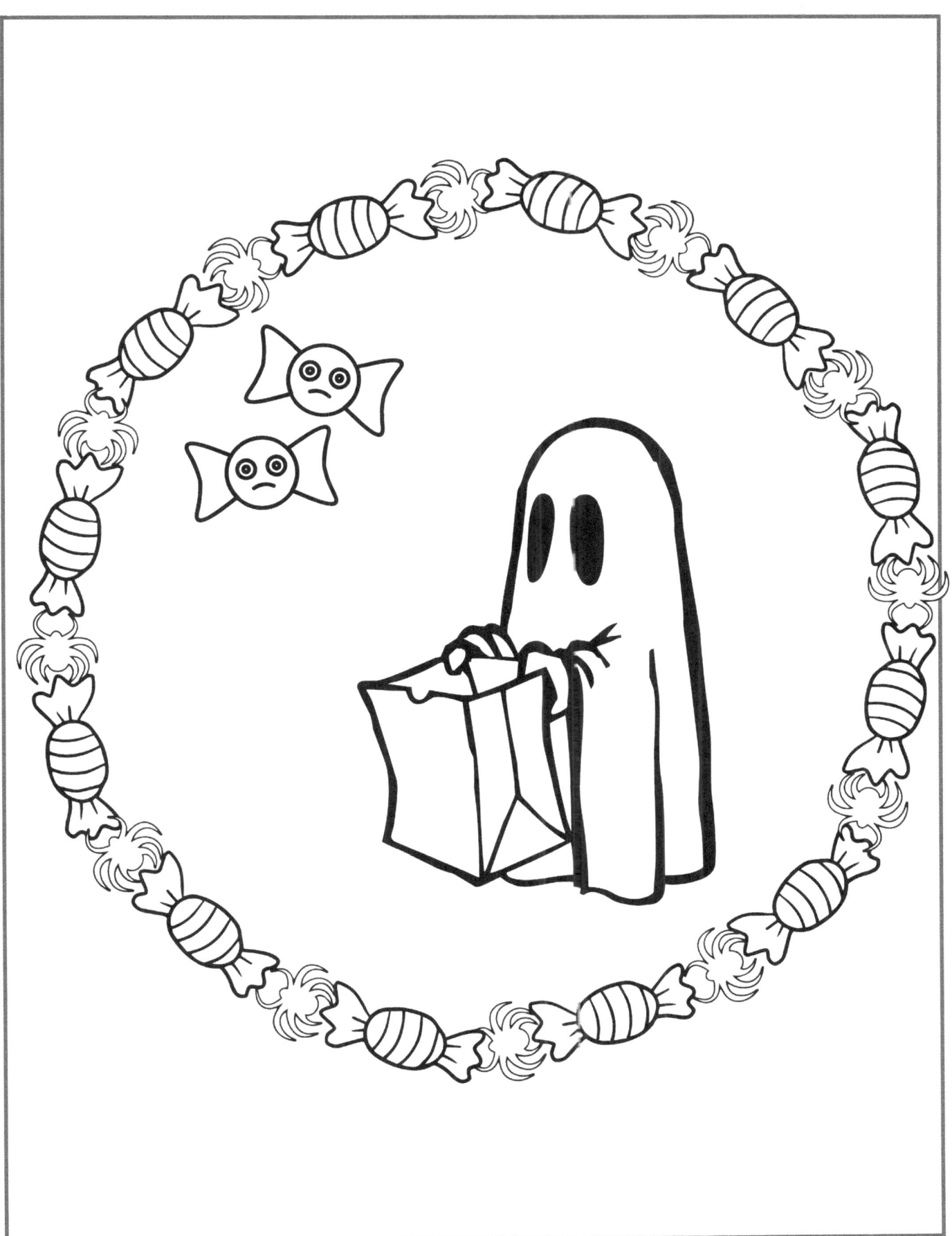

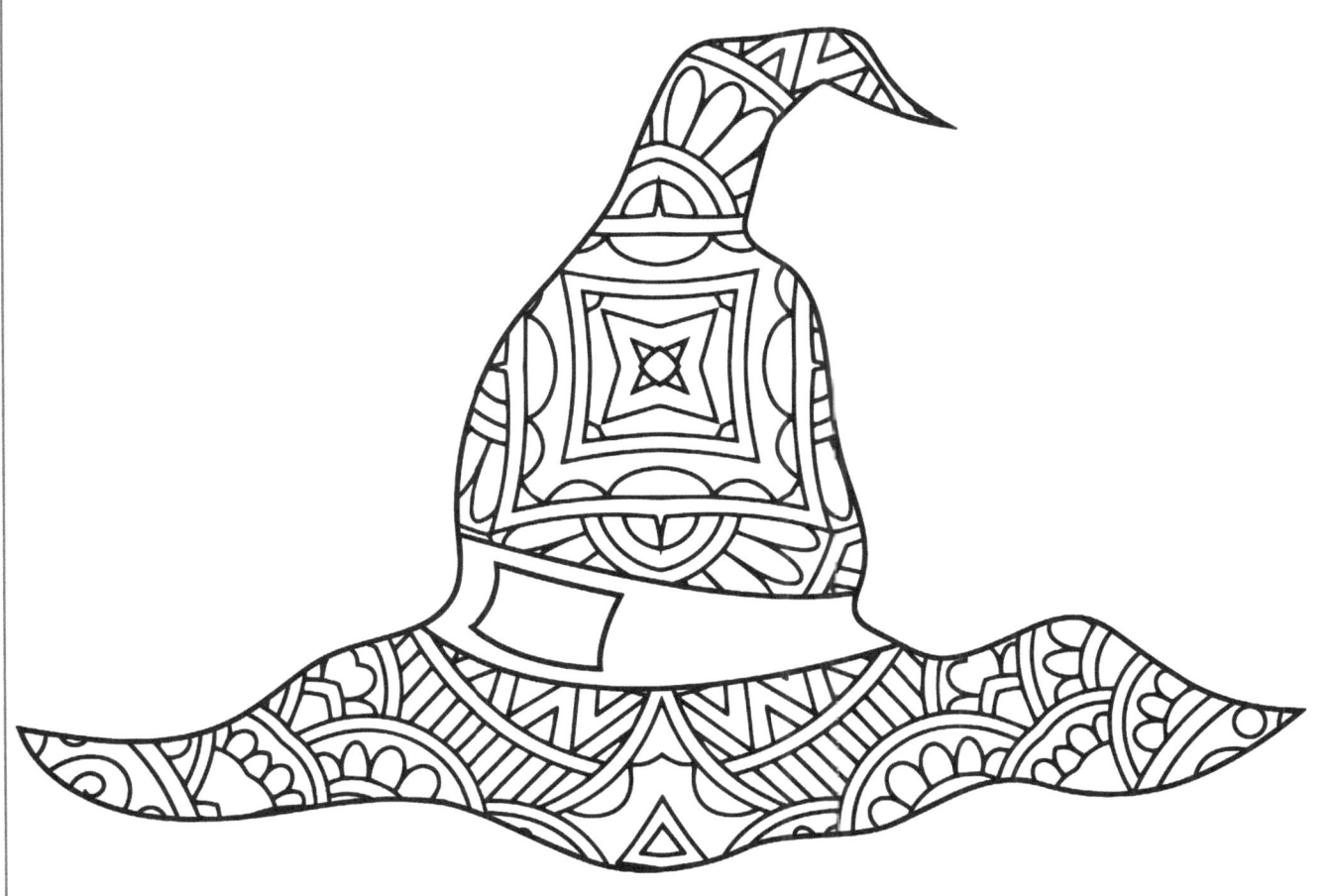

You say witch like it's a bad thing!

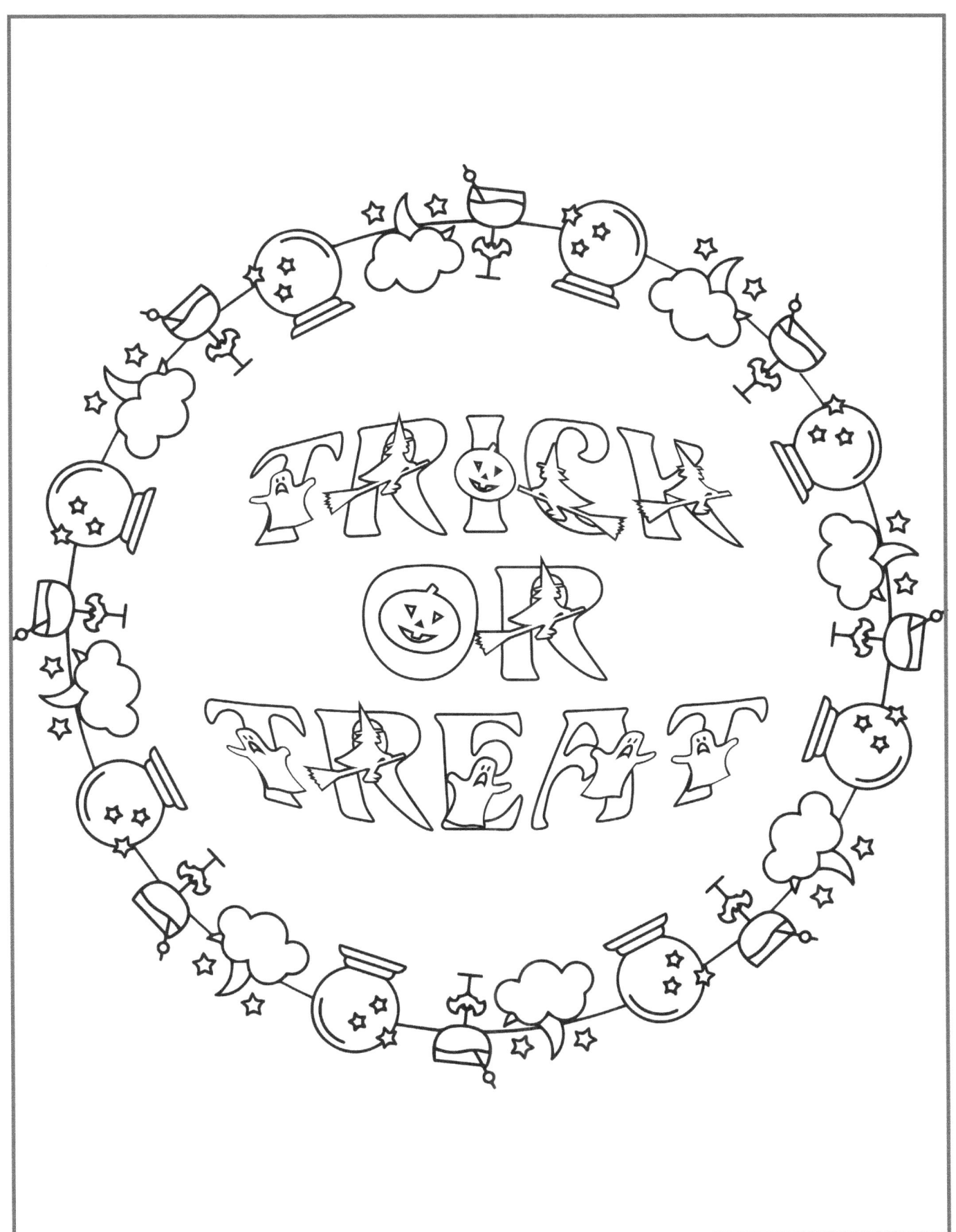

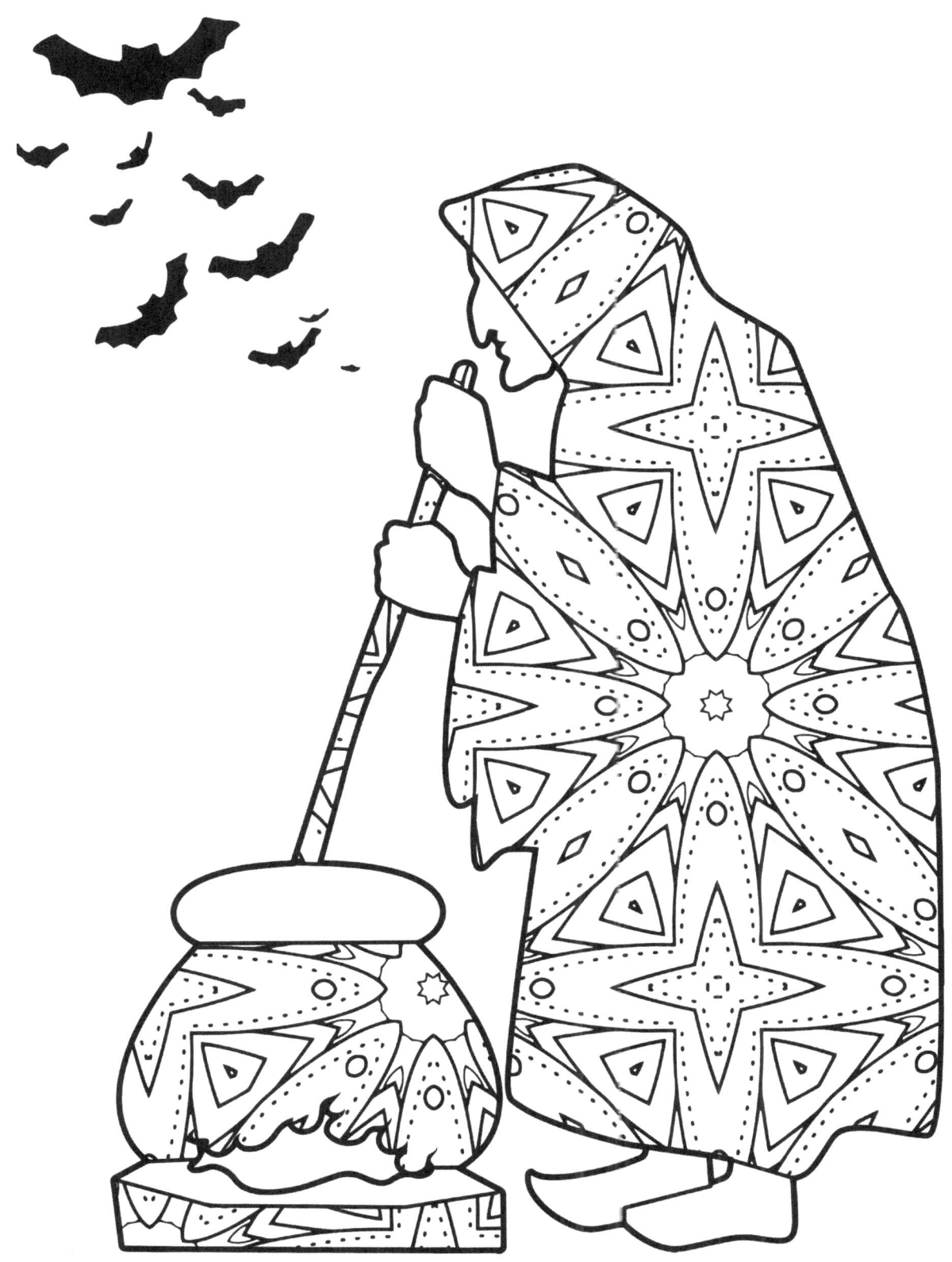

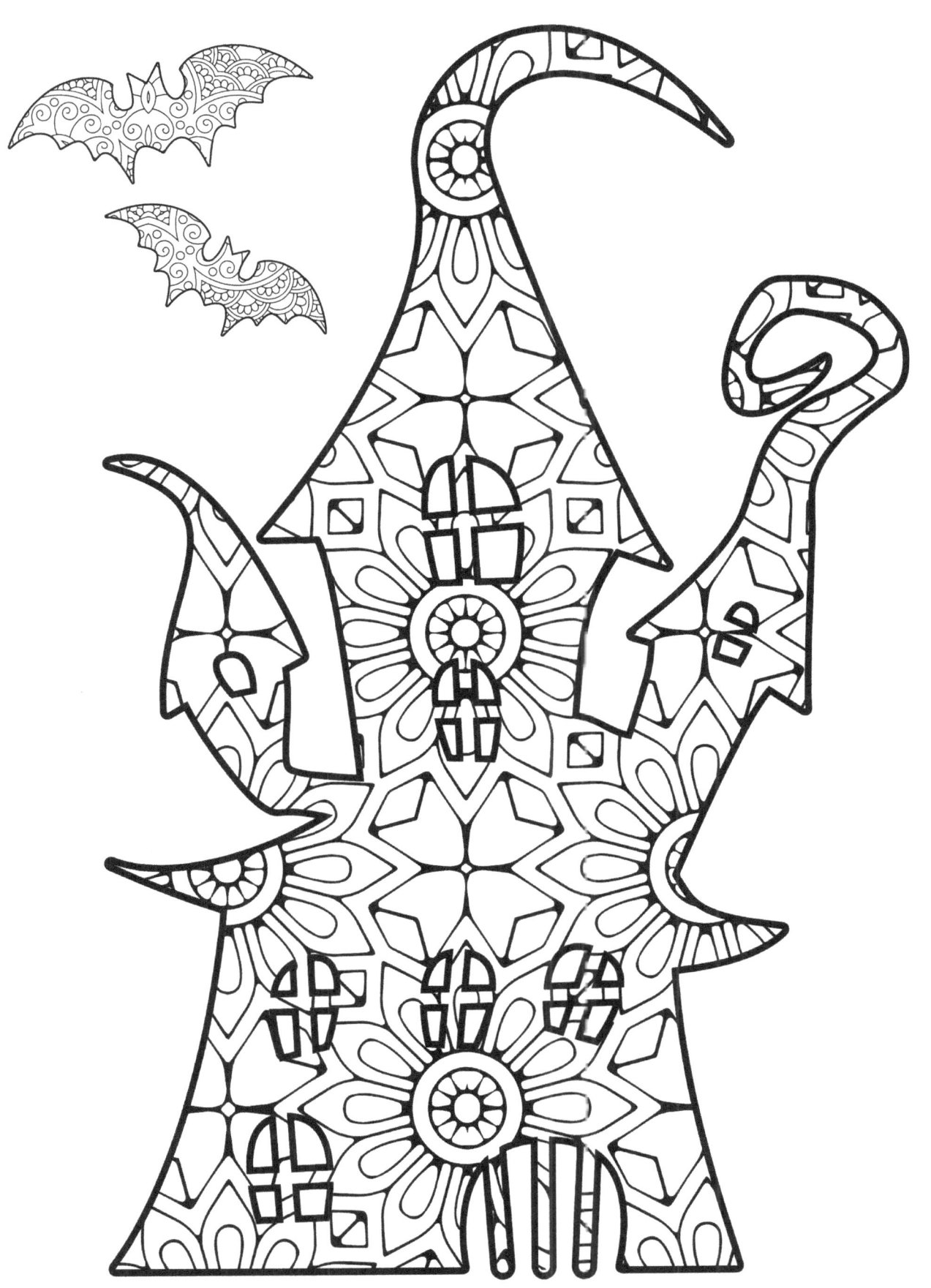

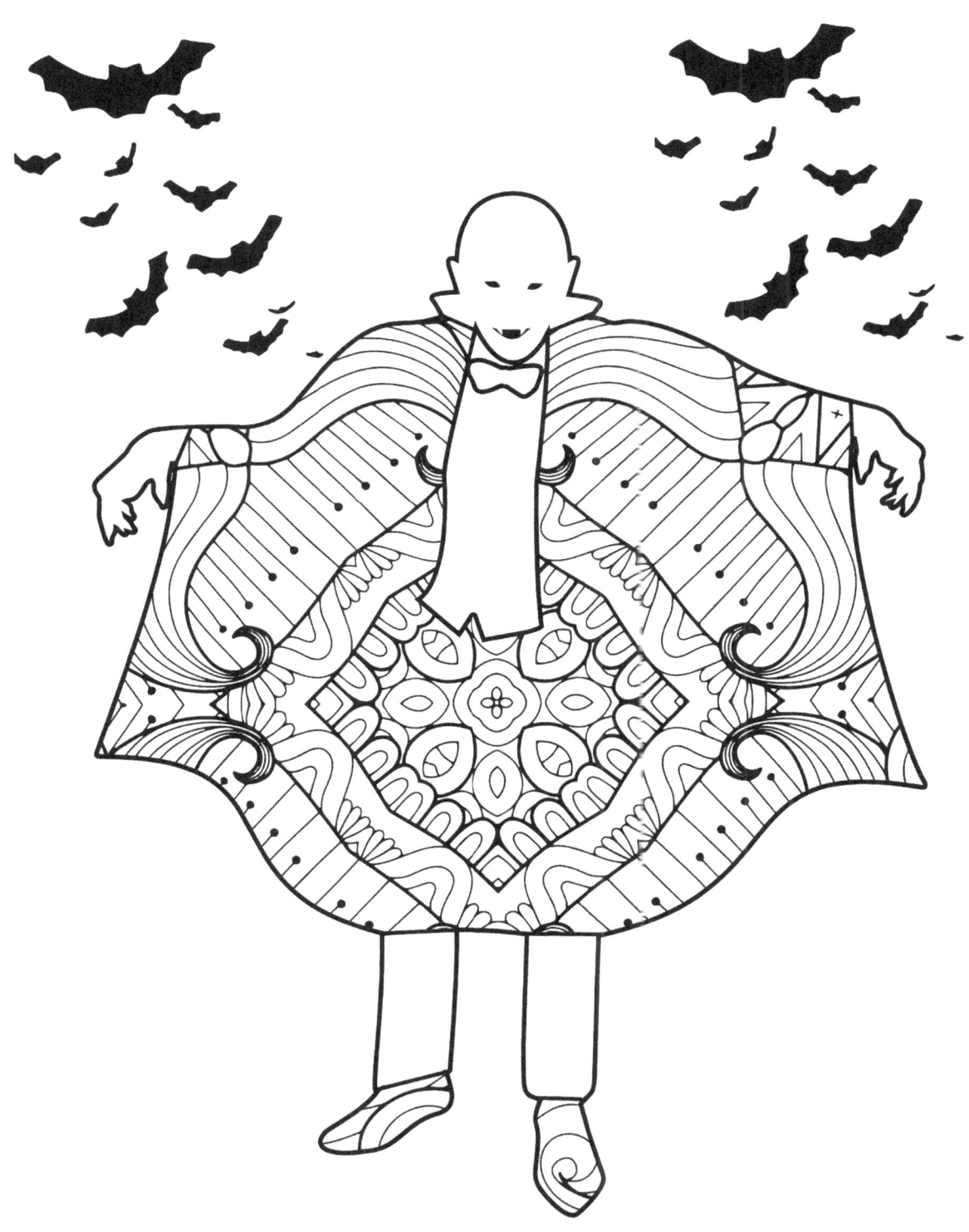

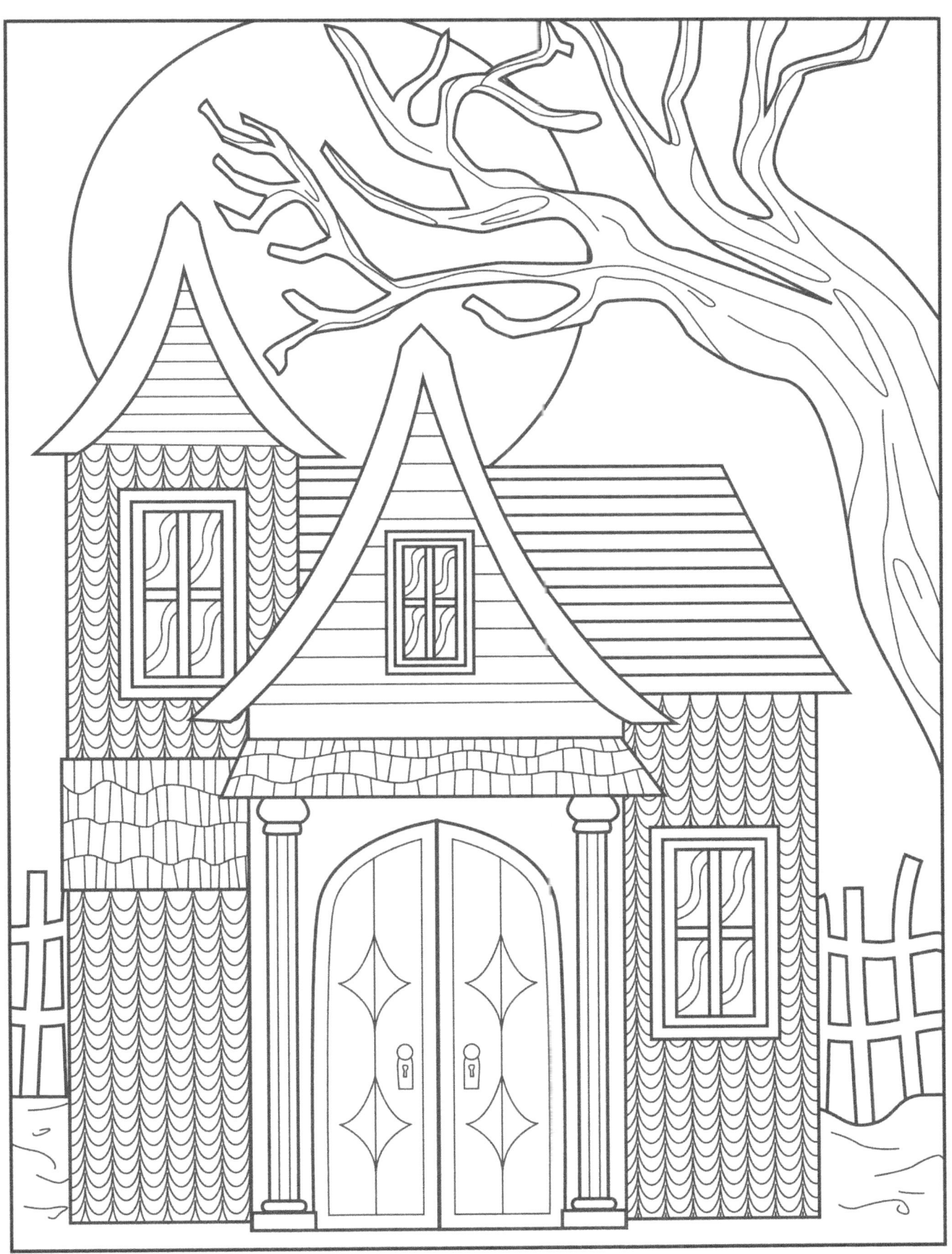

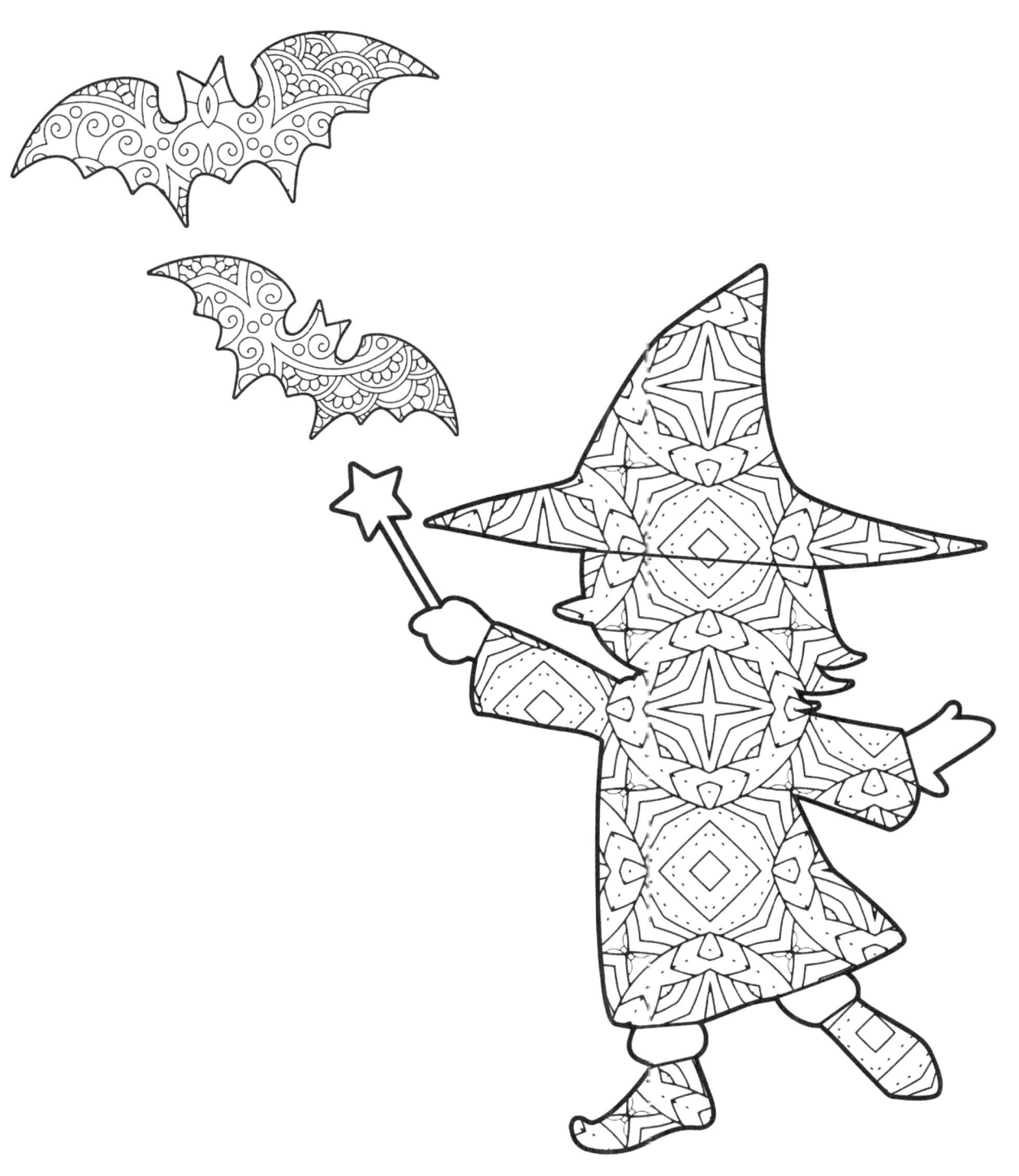

Double double toil and trouble: Fire burn, and caldron bubble"
William Shakespeare

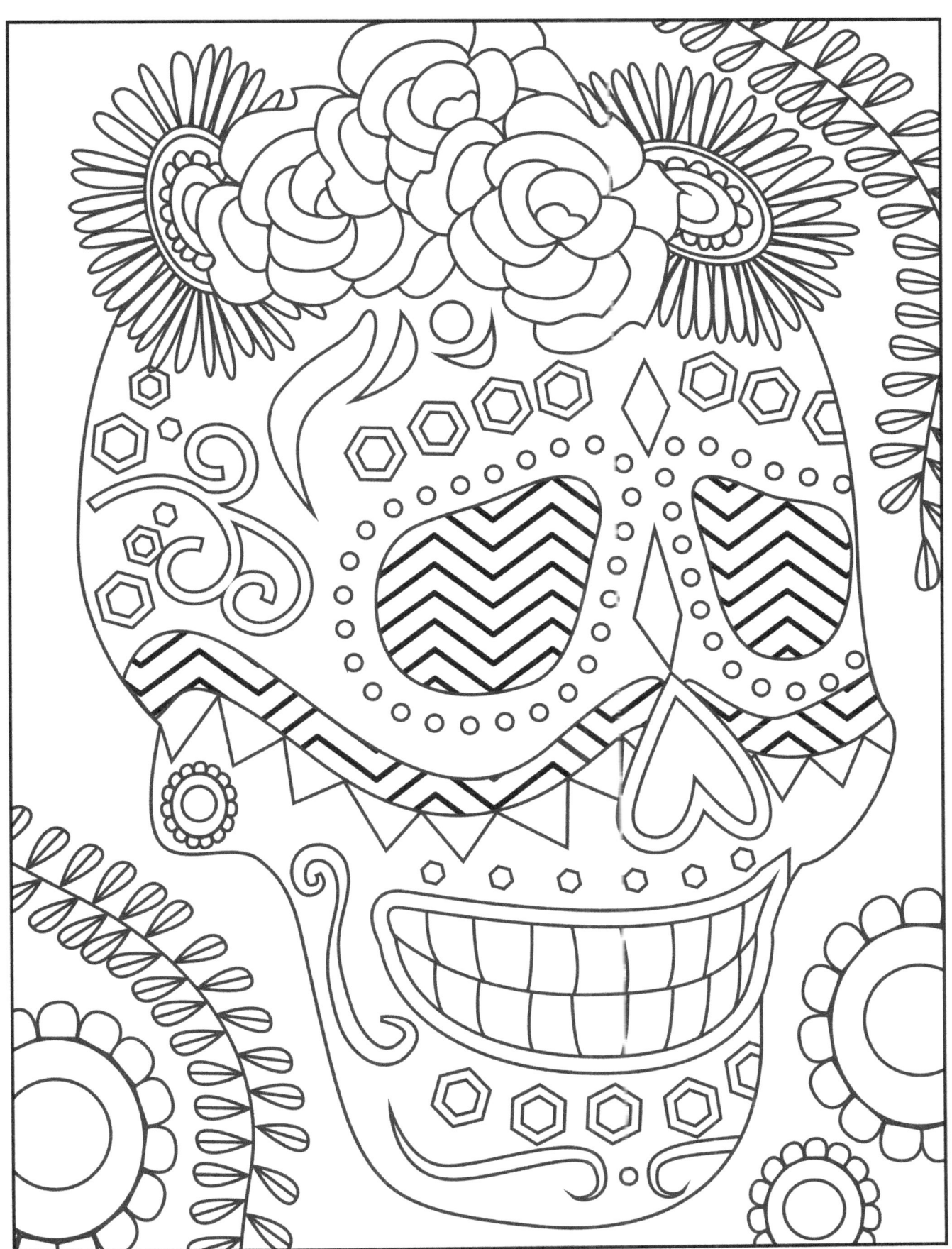

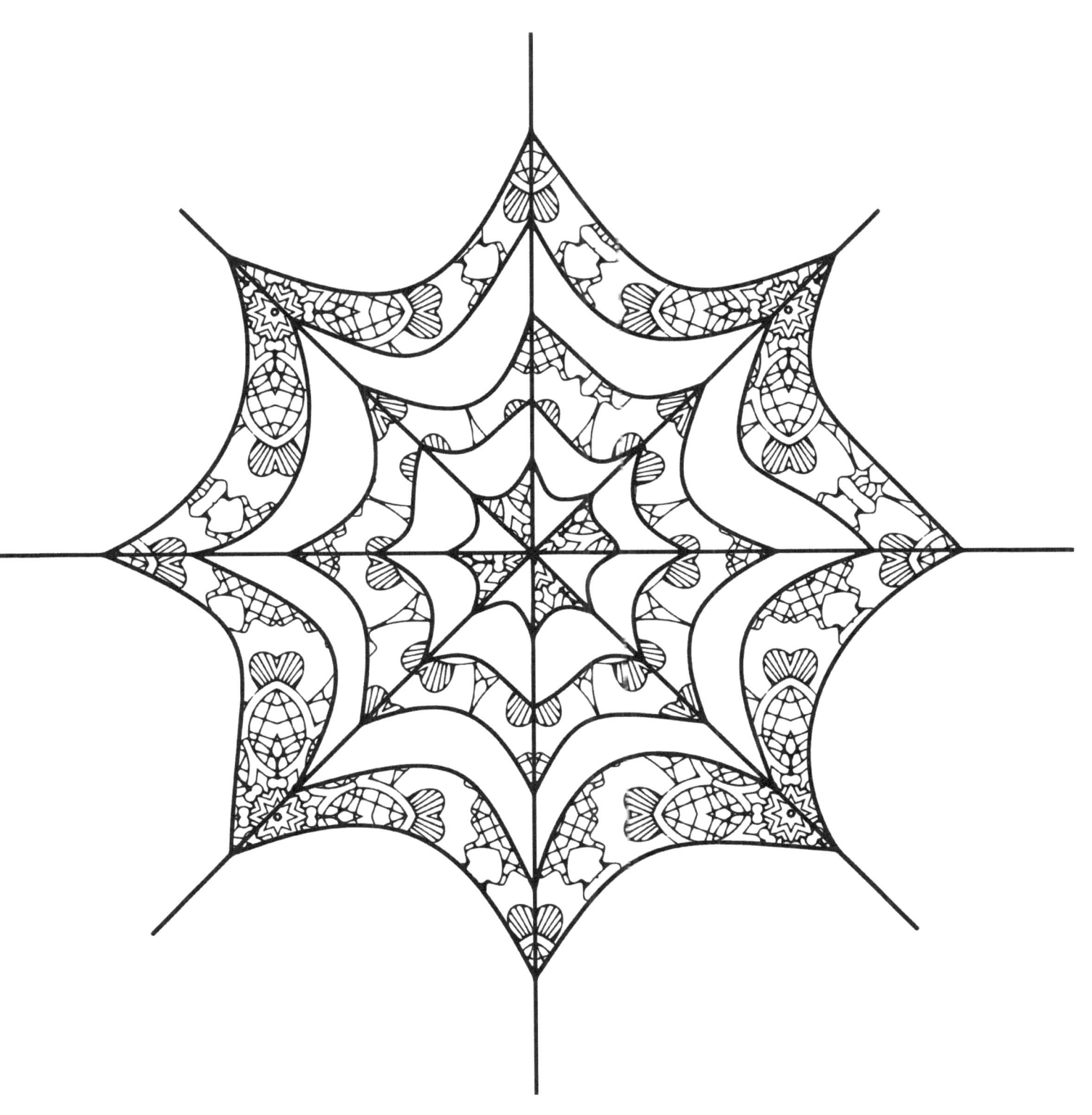

Witch and ghost make merry on this last of dear October's days

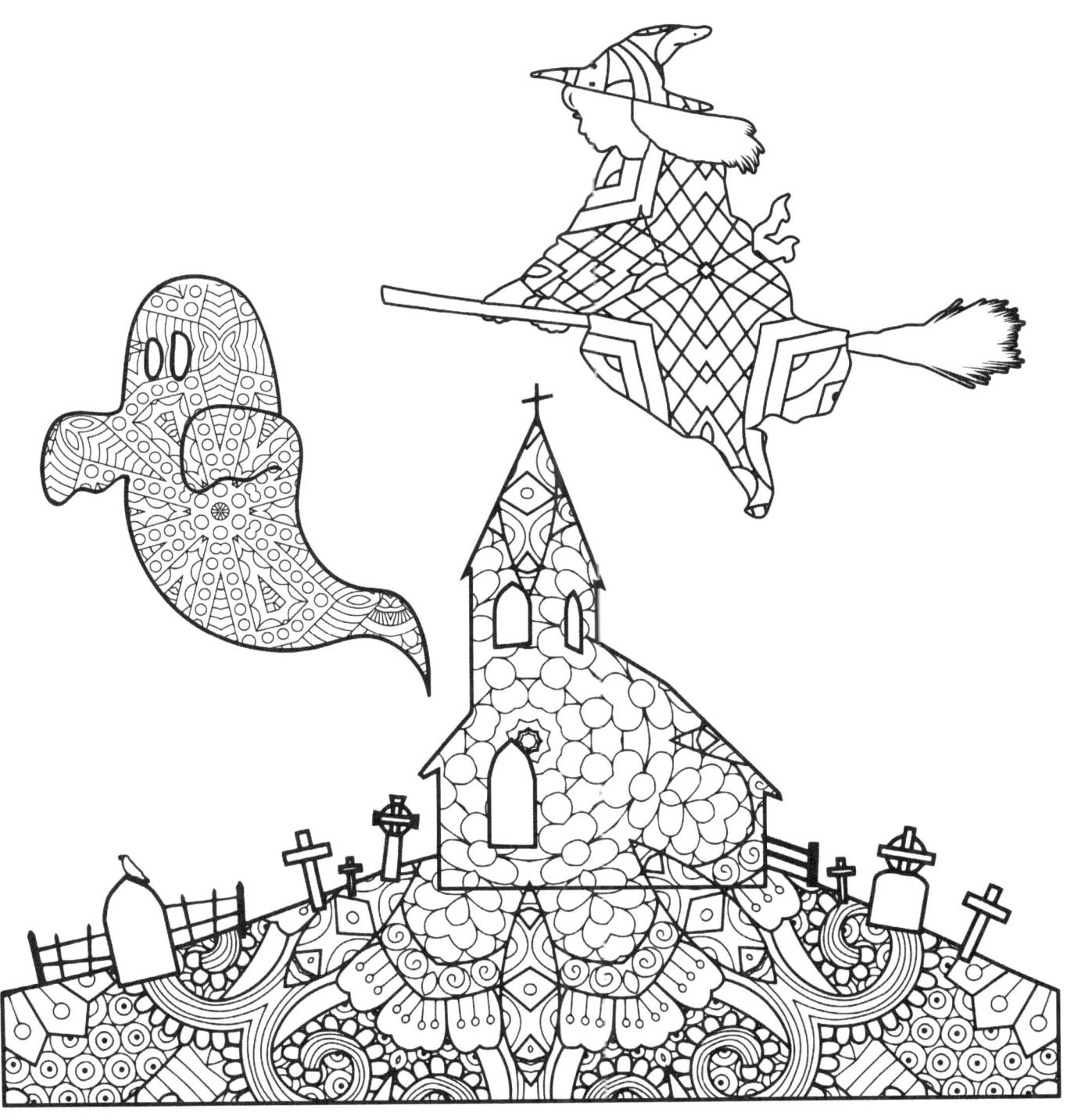

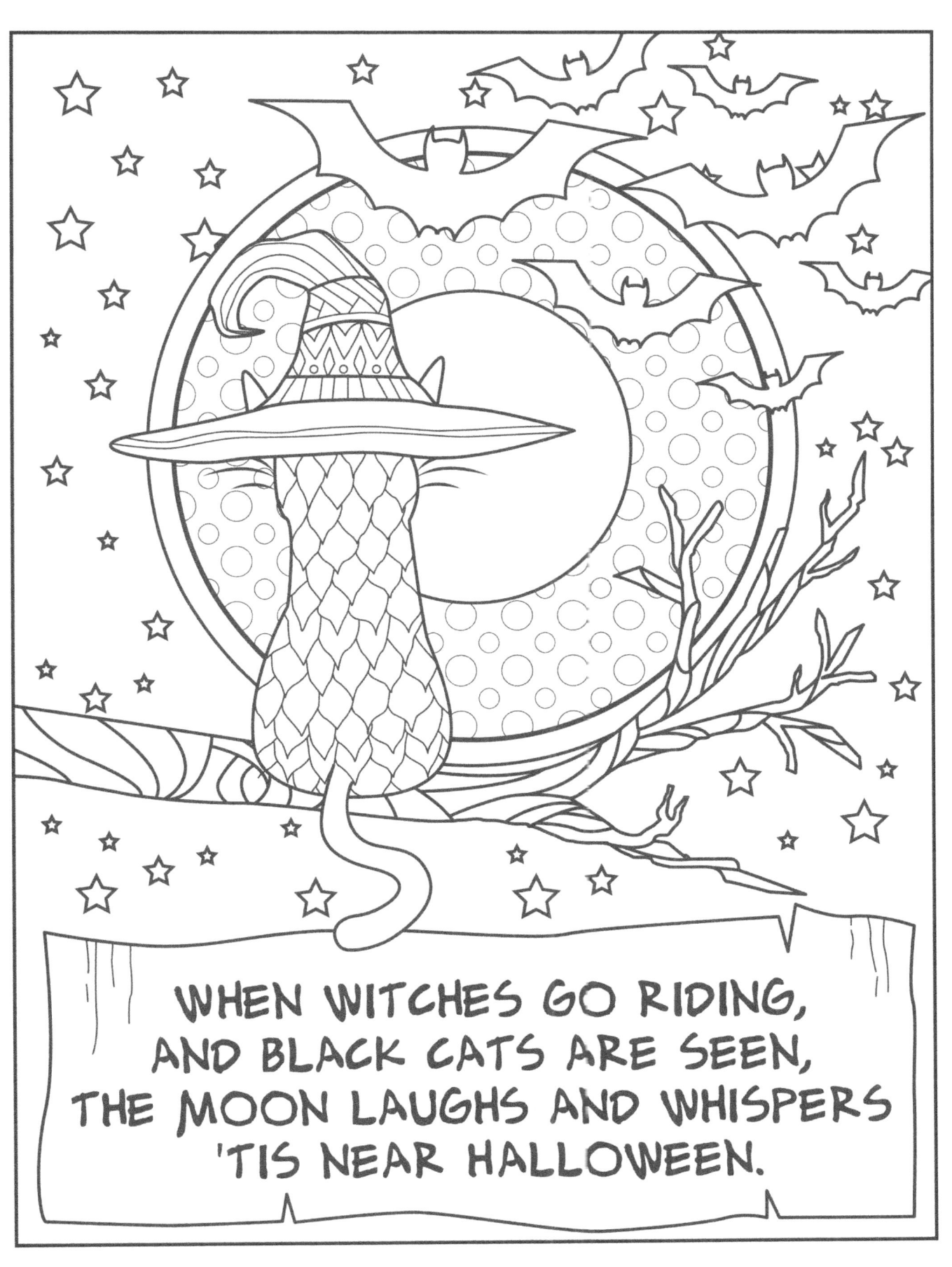

Wolves are silent
And the Moon is howling

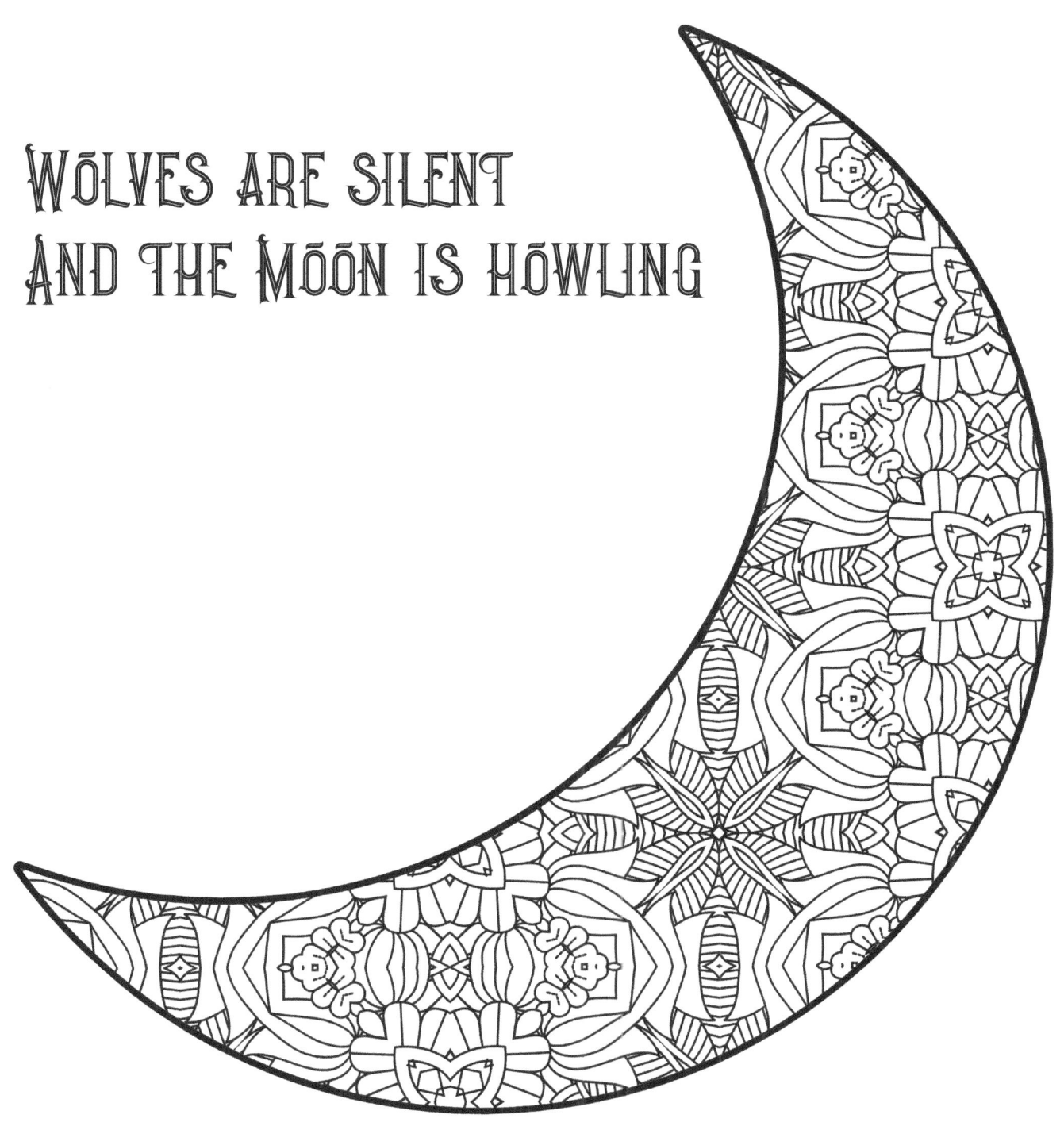

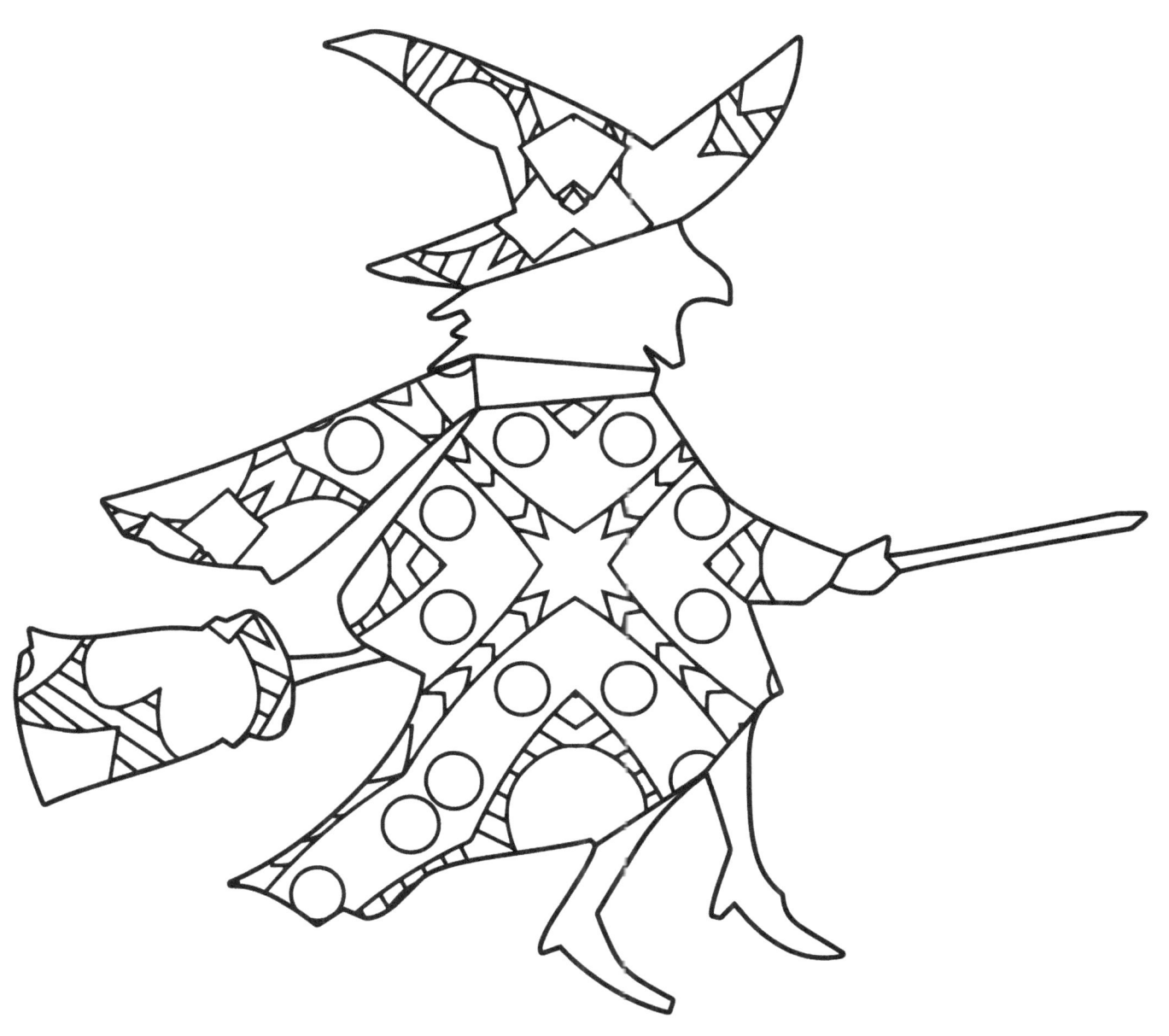

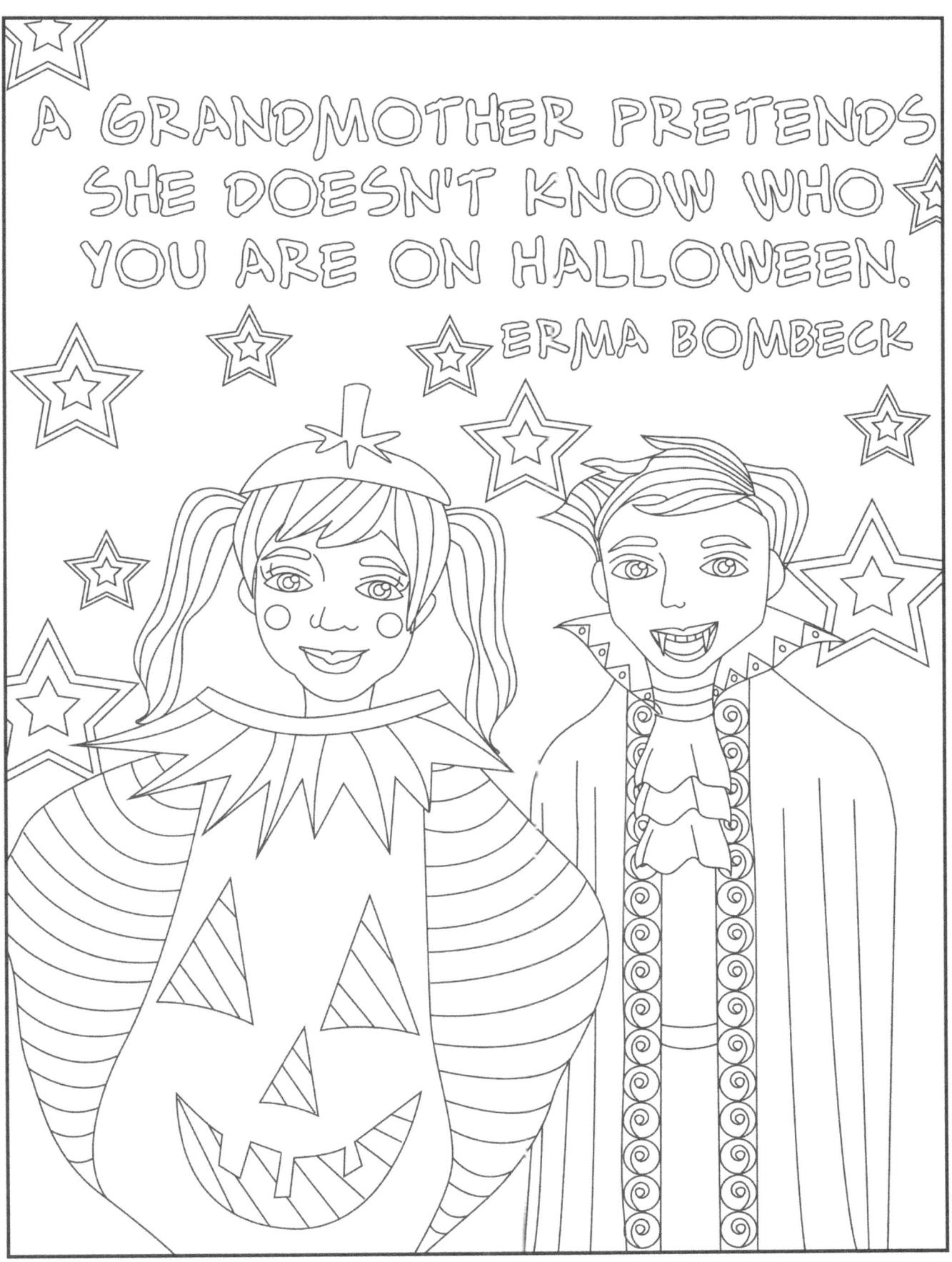

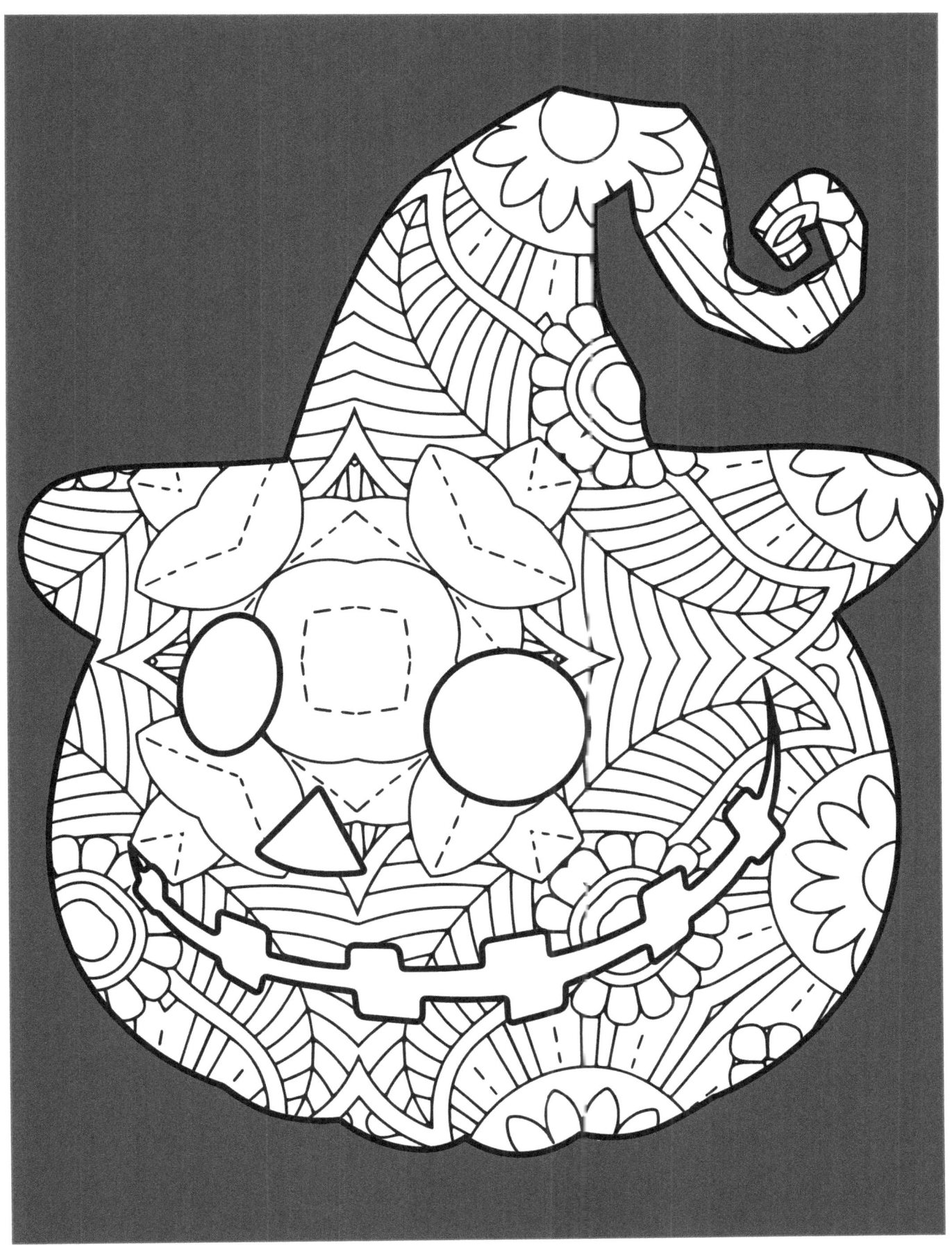

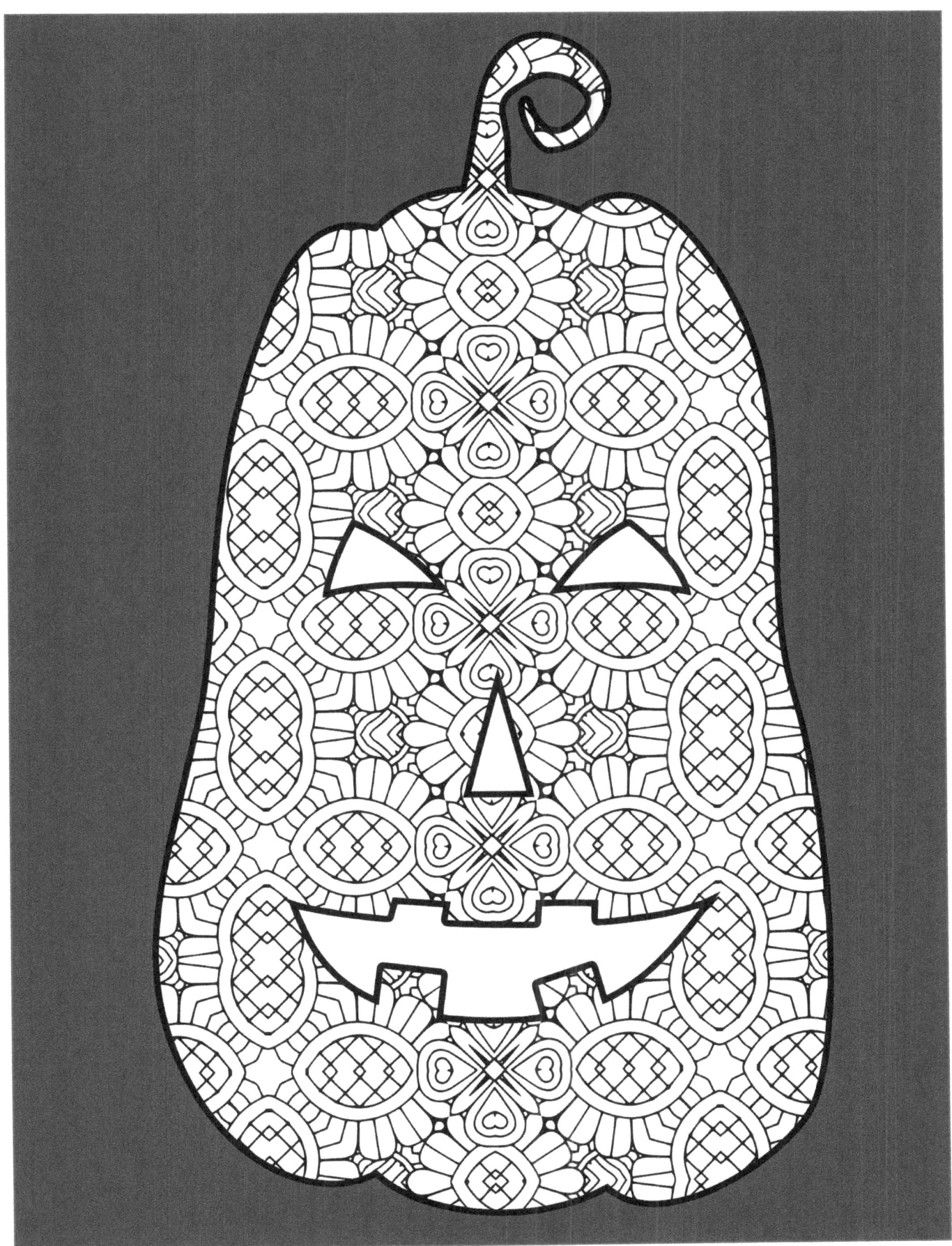

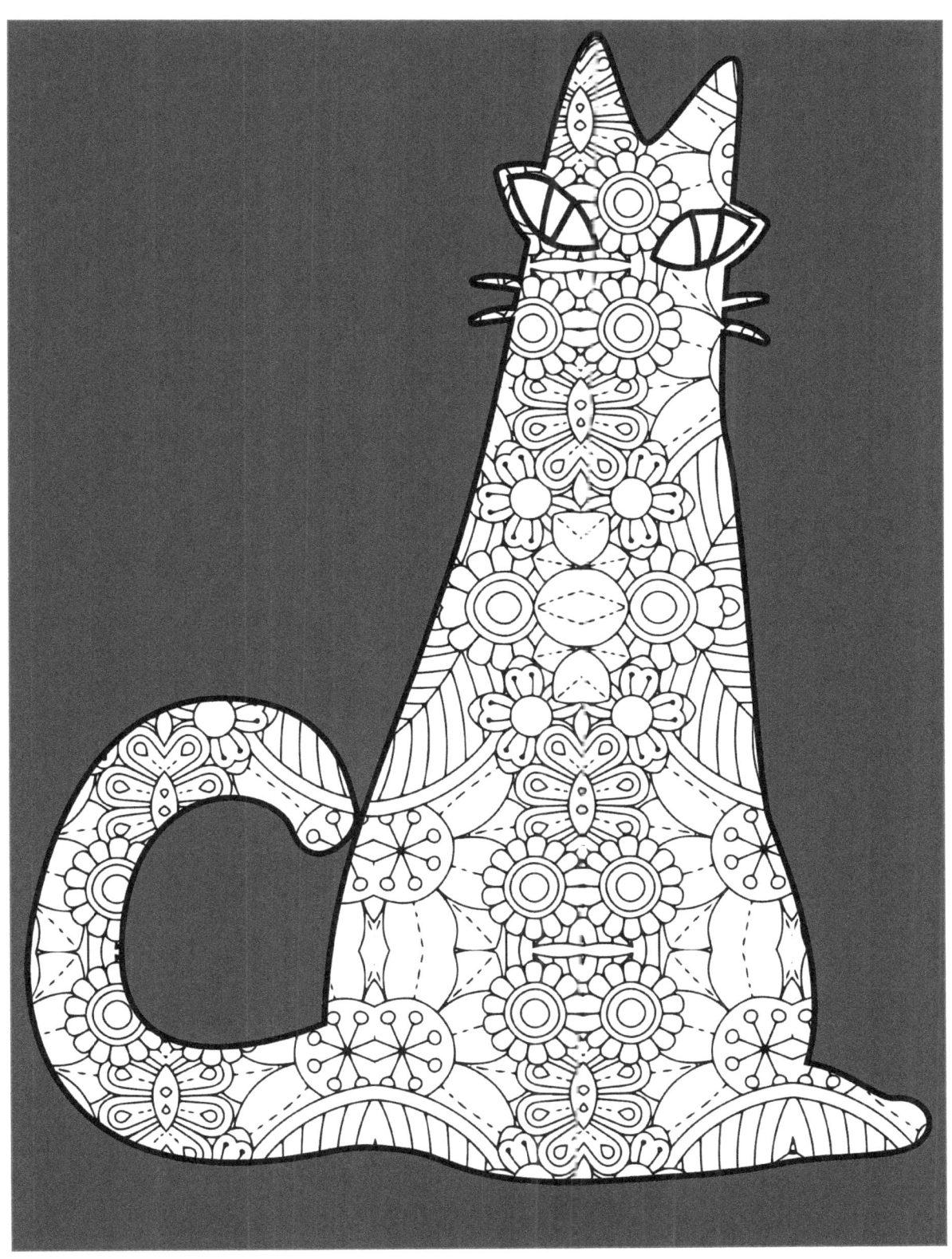

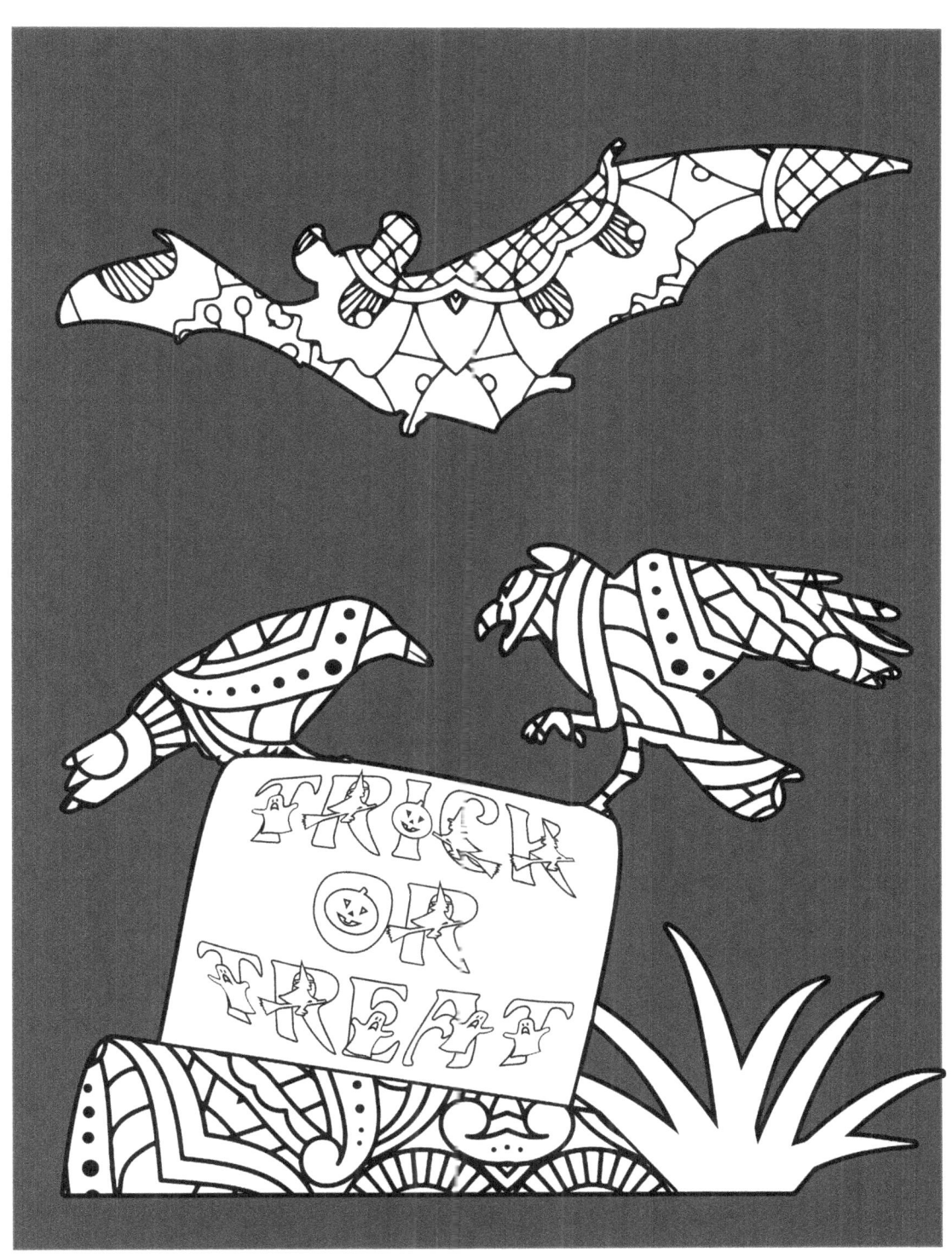

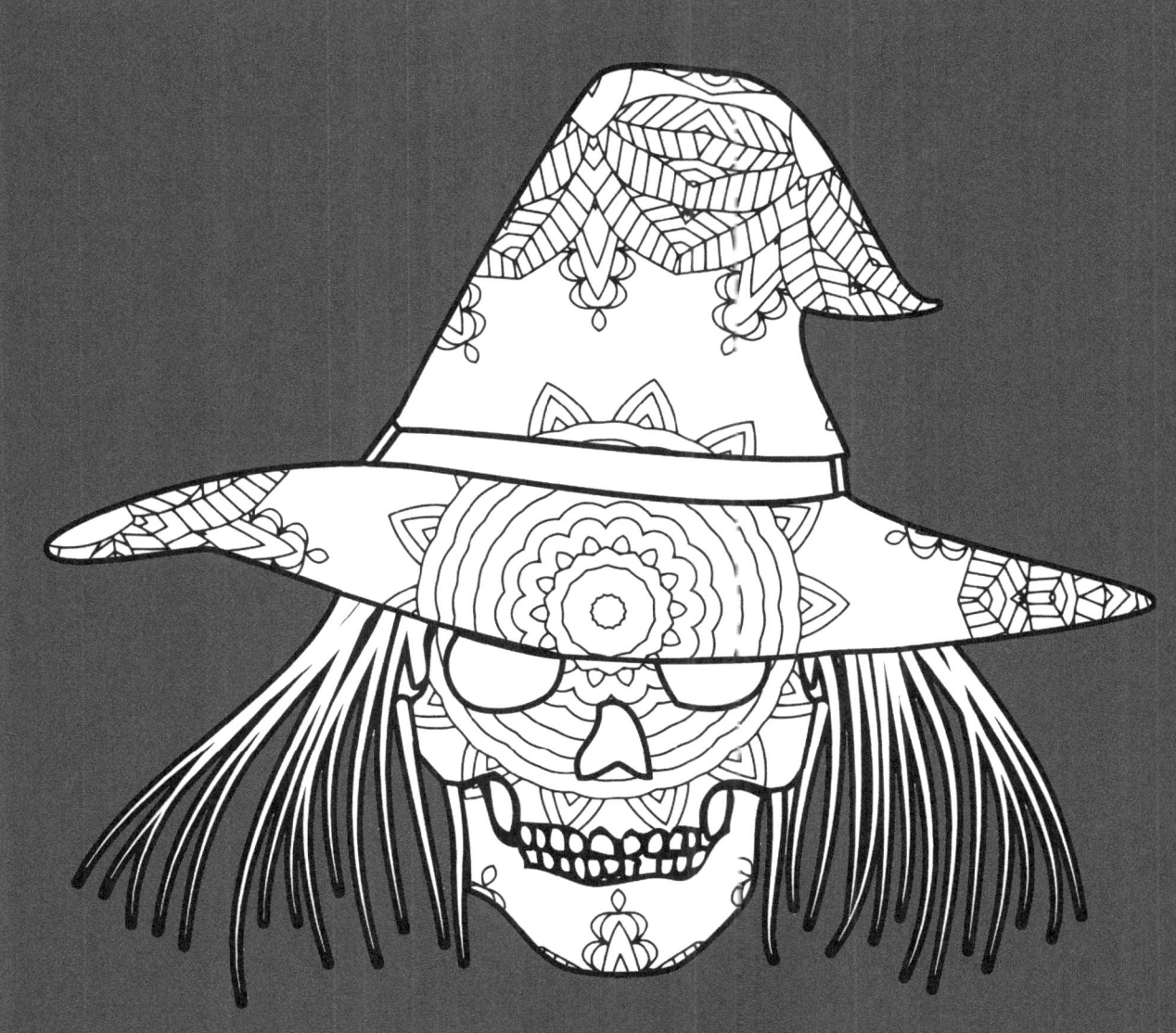

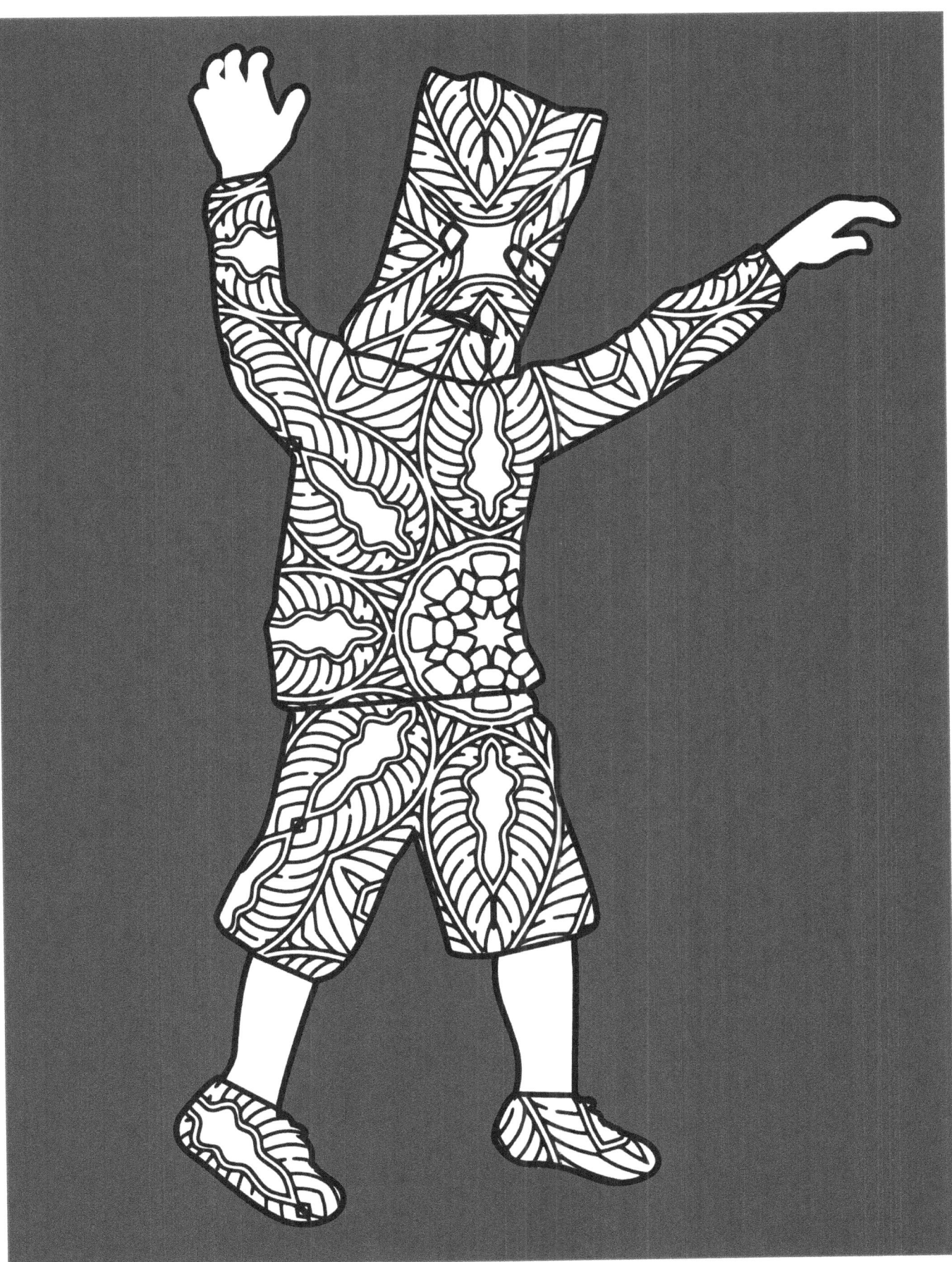

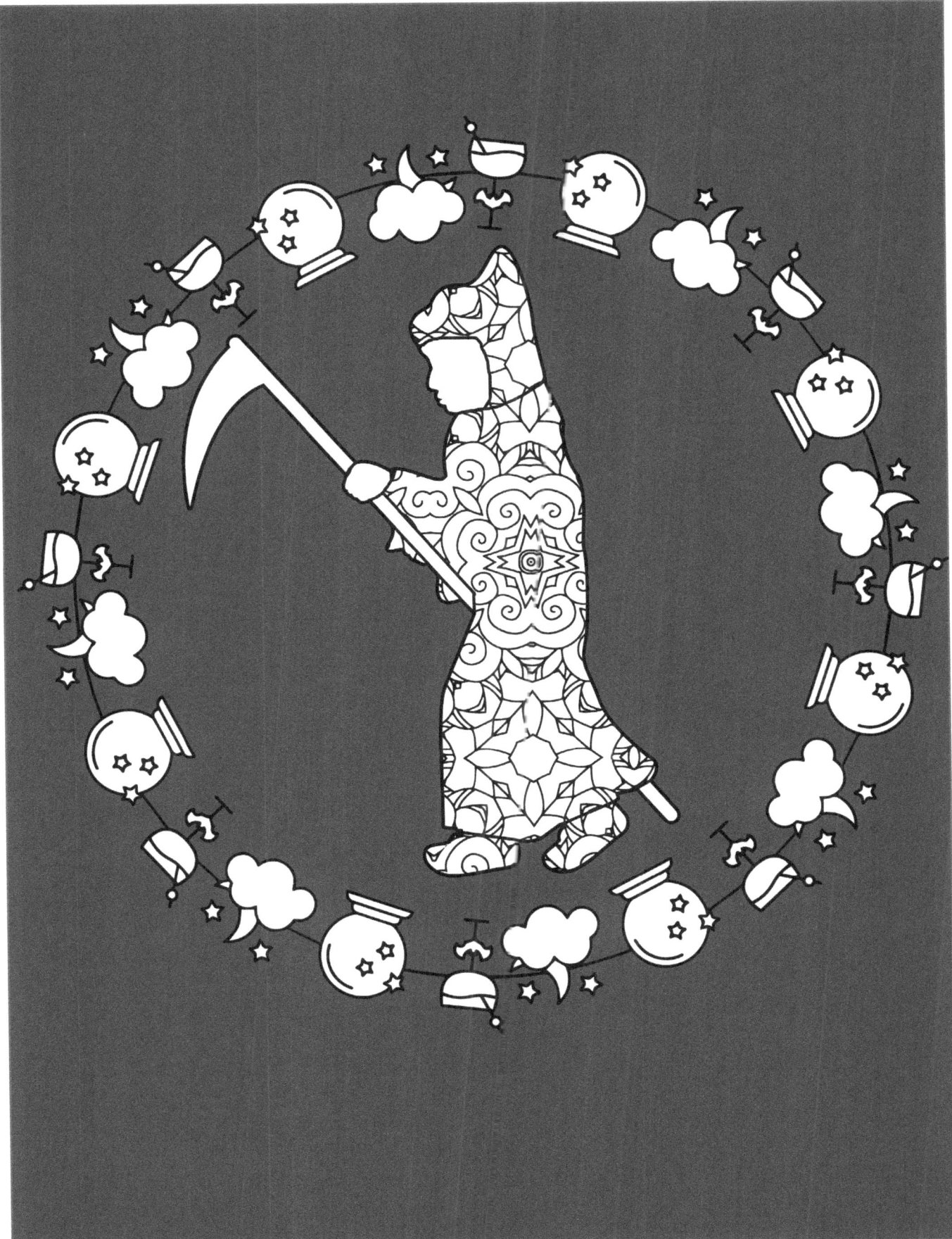

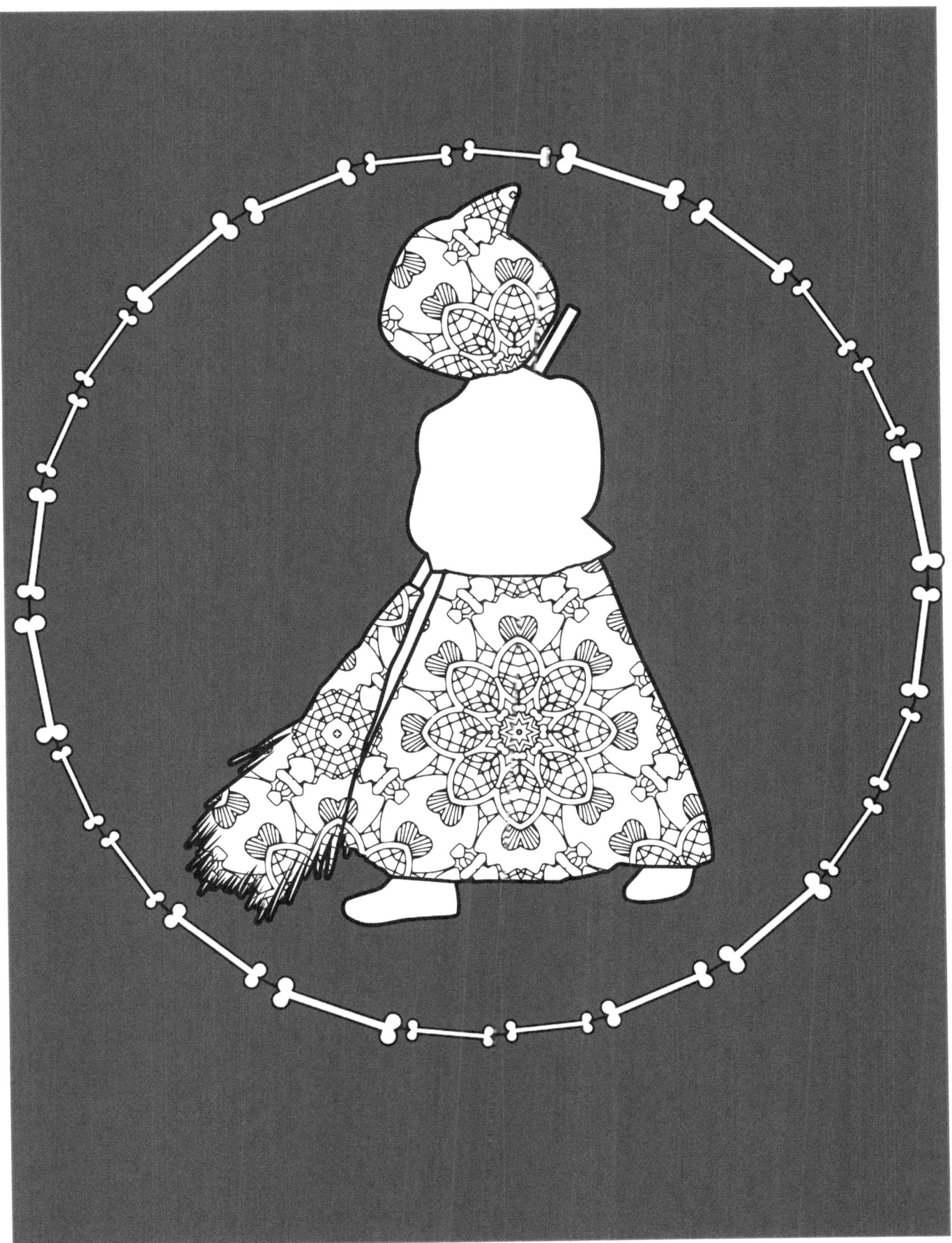

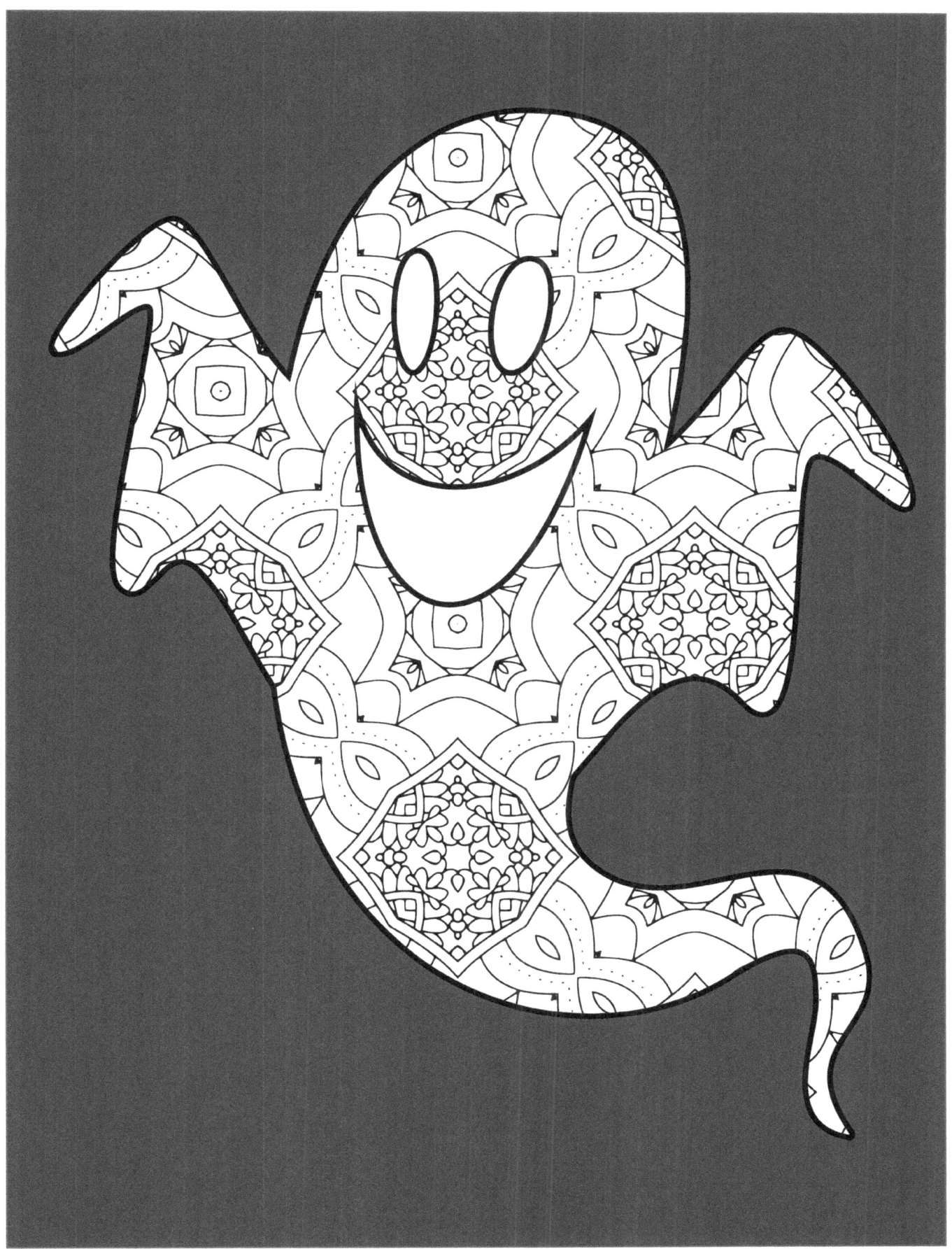

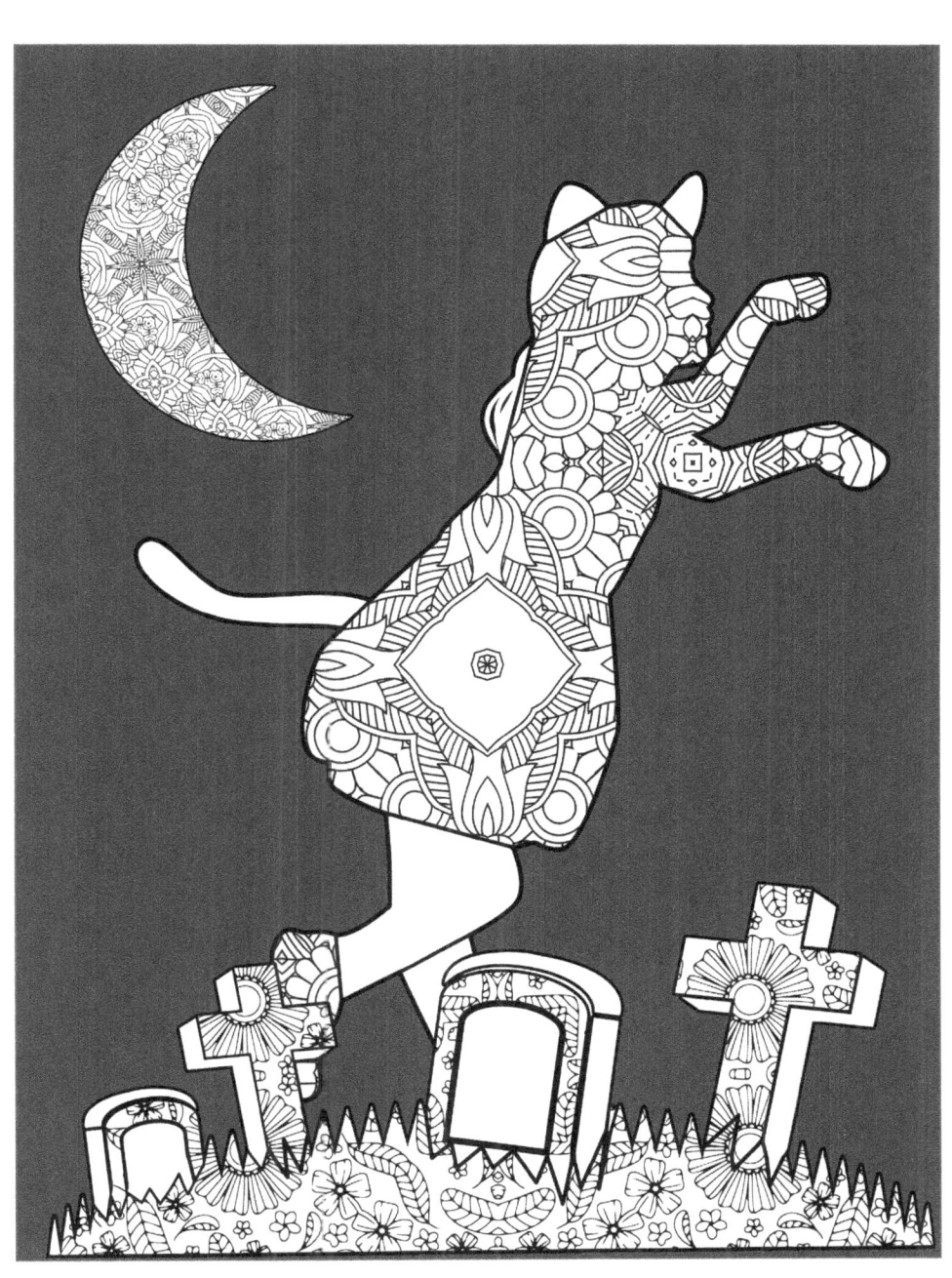

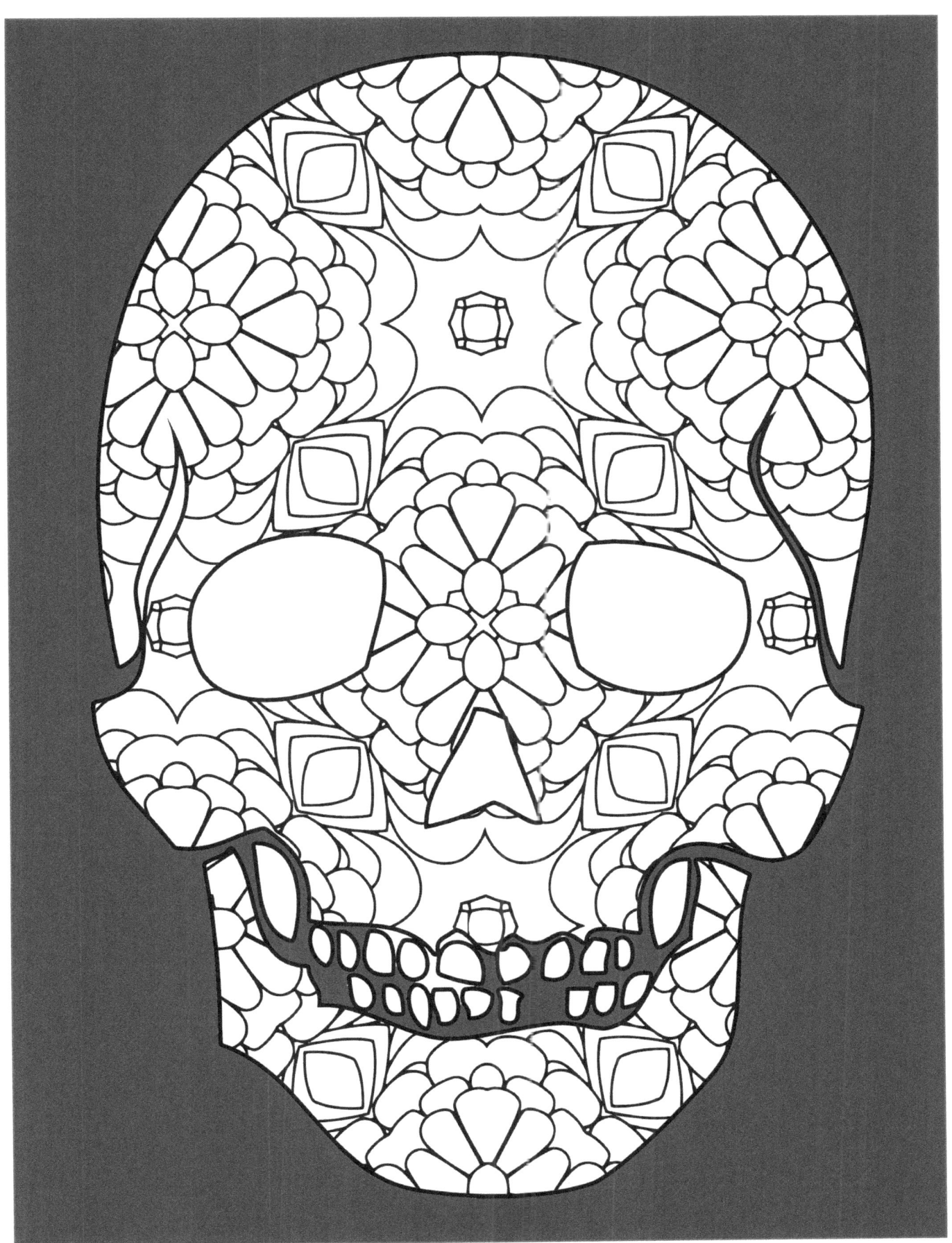

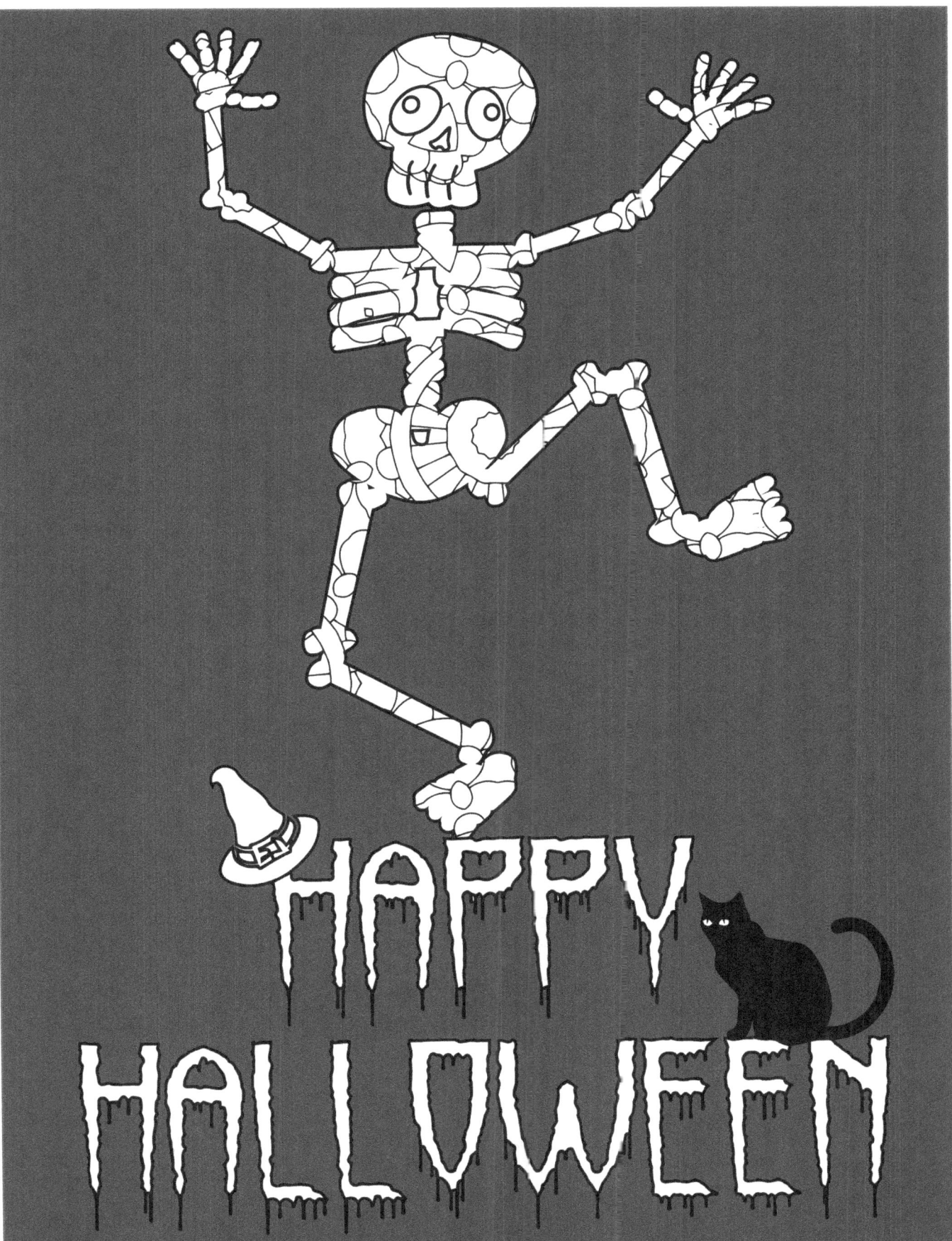

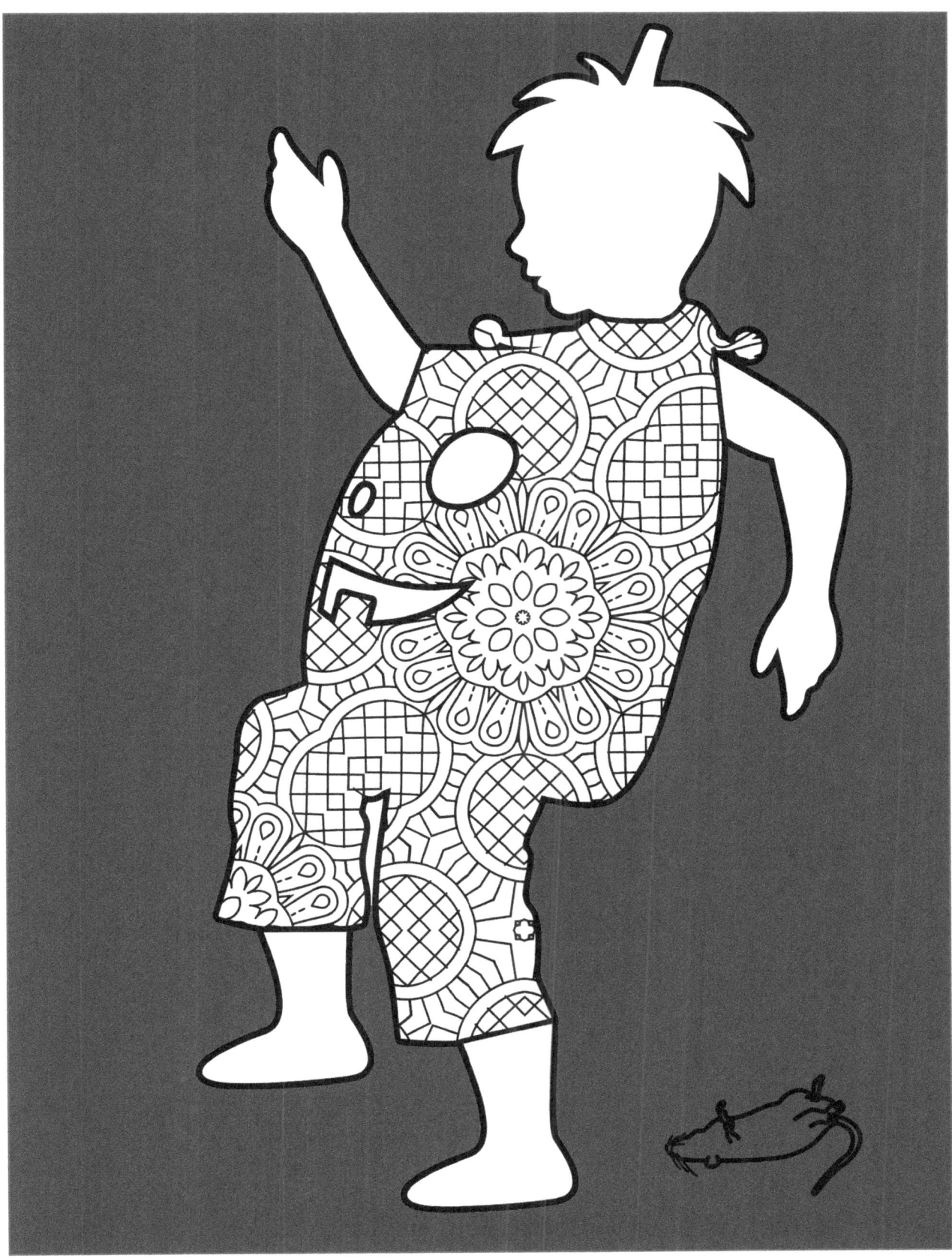

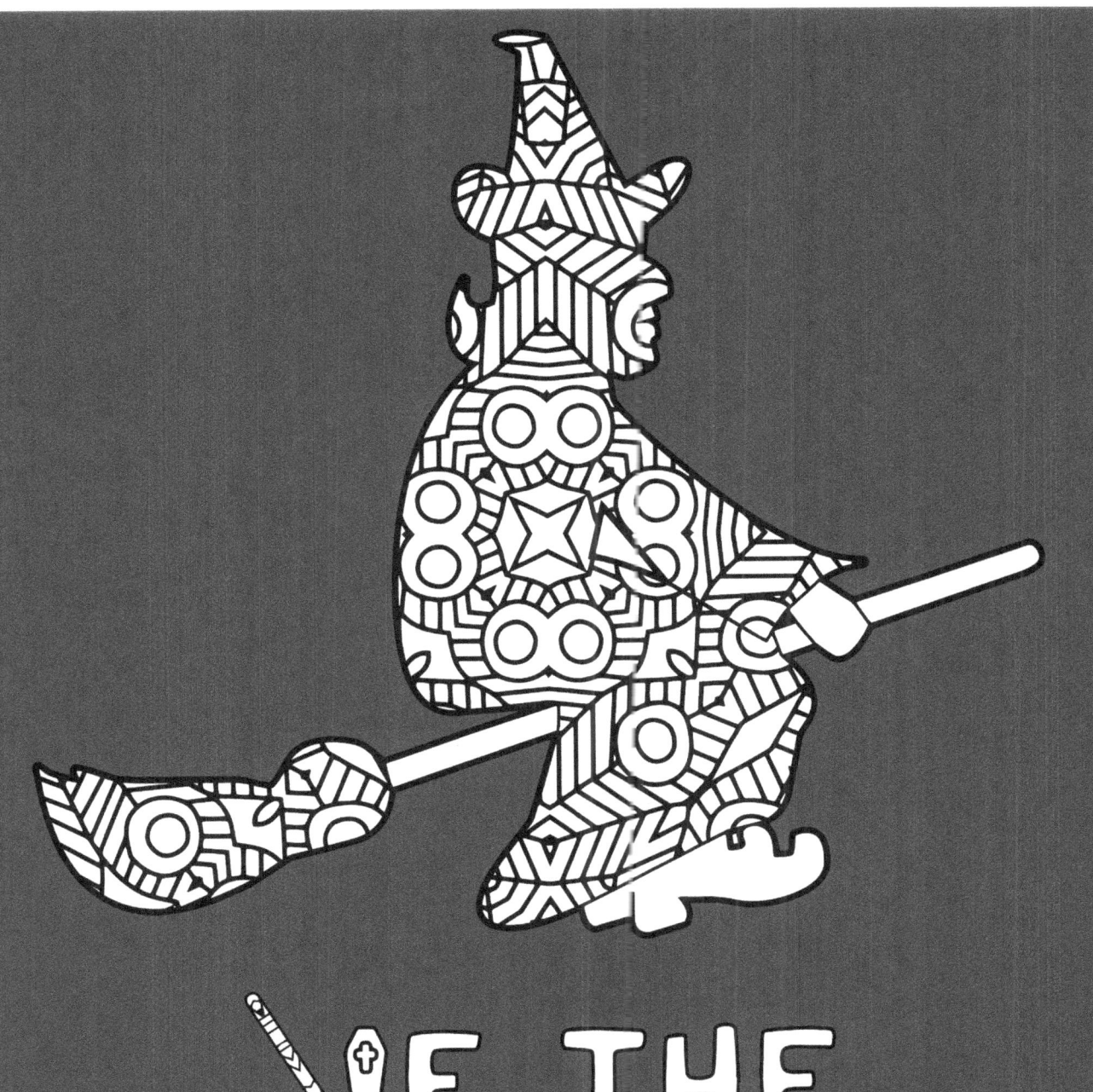

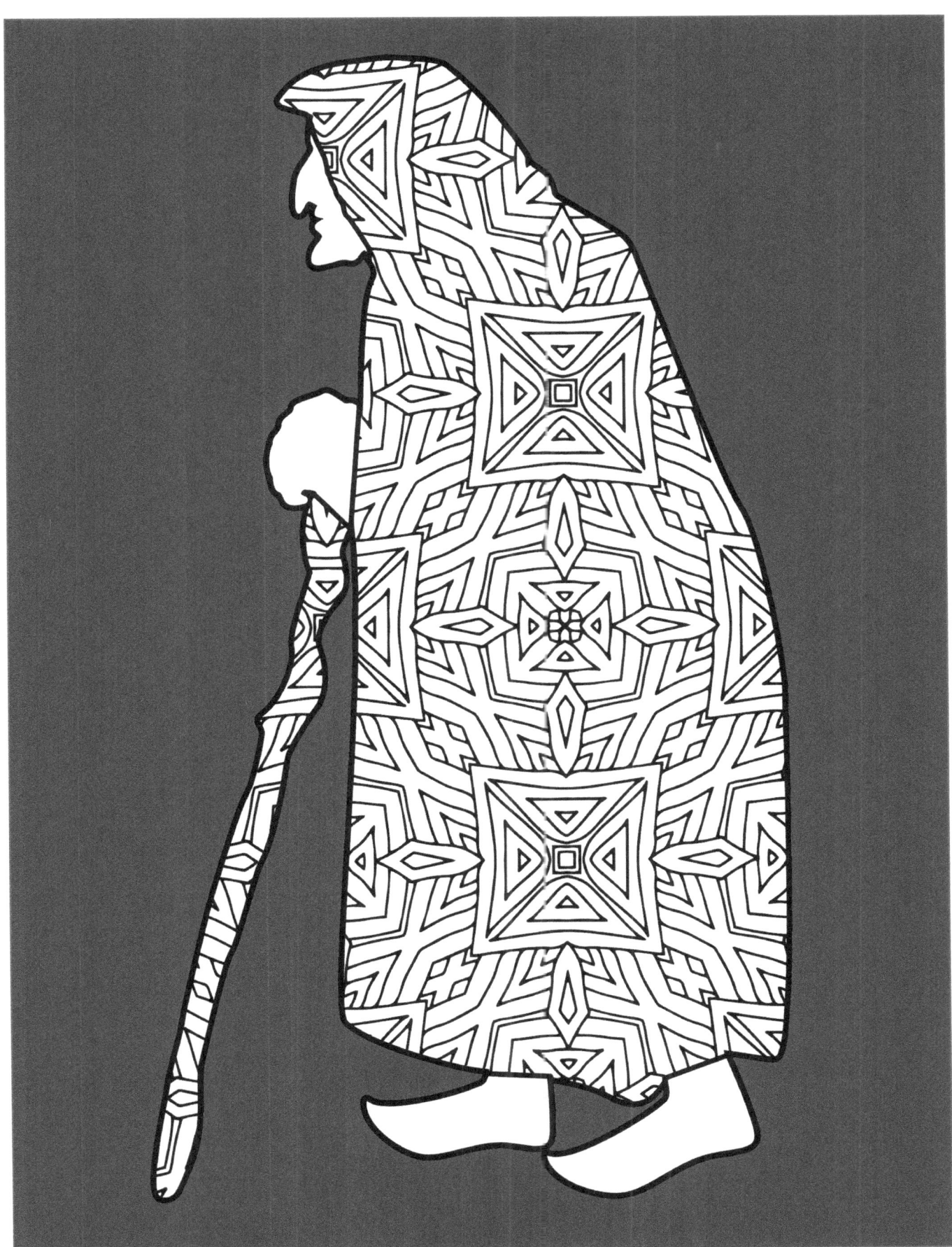

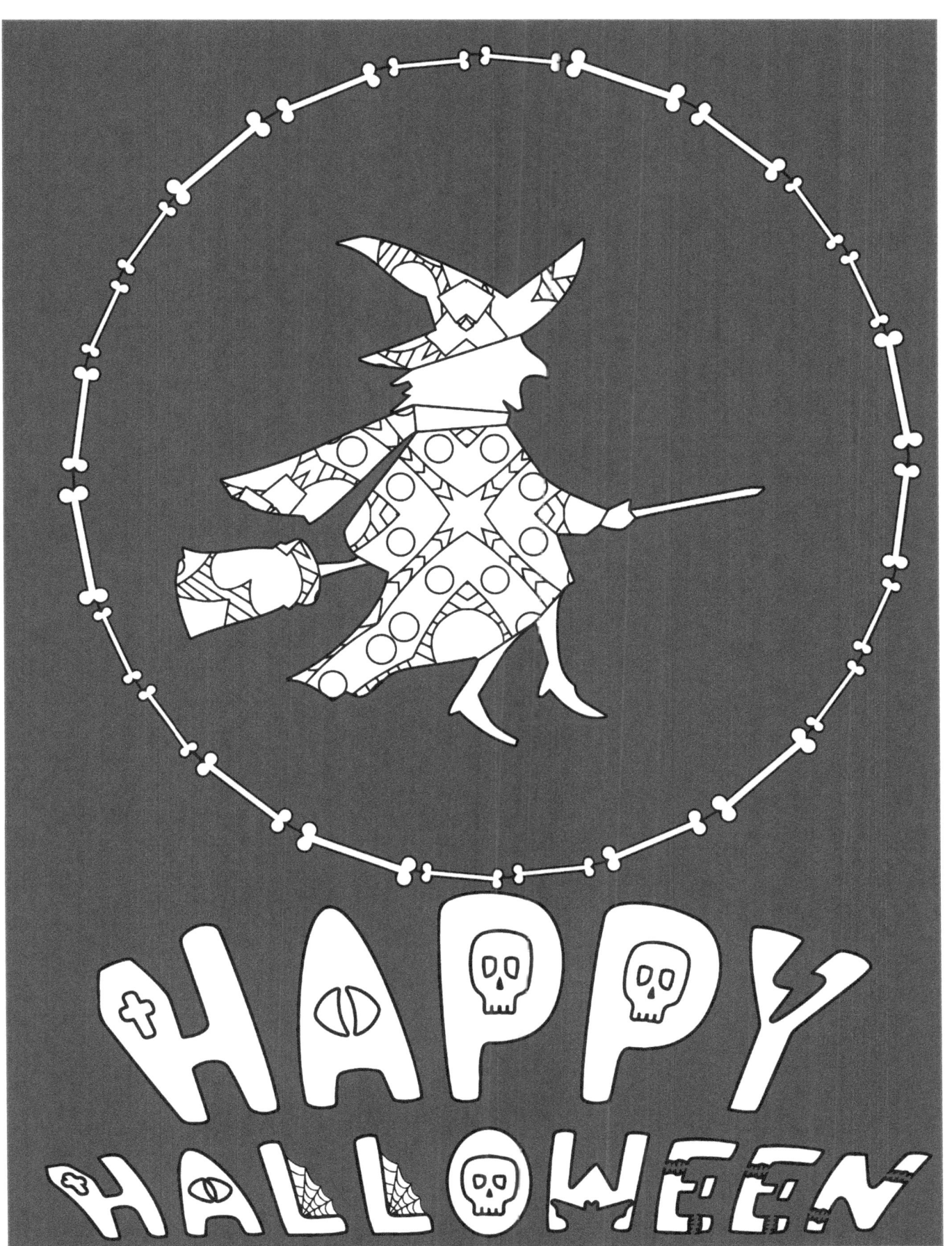

www.ingramcontent.com/pod-product-compliance
Lightning Source LLC
Chambersburg PA
CBHW080925220526
45465CB00008BA/2939